Obscenity and the Limits of Liberalism

OBSCENITY
and the Limits of Liberalism

edited by
LOREN GLASS and
CHARLES FRANCIS WILLIAMS

THE OHIO STATE UNIVERSITY PRESS • COLUMBUS

Library of Congress Cataloging-in-Publication Data
Obscenity and the limits of liberalism / edited by Loren Glass and Charles Francis Williams.
    p. cm.
Includes bibliographical references and index.
ISBN 978-0-8142-1172-4 (cloth : alk. paper)—ISBN 978-0-8142-9270-9 (cd)
    1. Obscenity (Law) 2. Freedom of expression. 3. Liberalism—History. I. Glass, Loren
Daniel. II. Williams, Charles Francis, 1970– III. Title.

    K5293.O27 2011
    342.08'5—dc23

Cover design by Janna Thompson-Chordas
Text design by Juliet Williams
Type set in ITC New Baskerville
Printed by Thomson-Shore, Inc.

9   8   7   6   5   4   3   2   1

Contents

Acknowledgments

First and foremost, we would like to thank Jay Semel, Director of the Obermann Center for Advanced Studies, along with his staff—Jennifer New, Karla Tonella, and Carolyn Frisbie—for all their support and assistance in organizing the Humanities Symposium at which the contributions to this collection originated. "Obscenity: An Interdisciplinary Discussion," held March 1–4, 2007, on the campus of the University of Iowa, included not only conventional panels but also performances, screenings, art exhibits, and radio shows. The promotion and coordination of all these events would have been impossible without the funding and support of the Obermann Center and its staff, whose contributions to interdisciplinary scholarship at the University of Iowa have been invaluable. Our program committee—Rob Latham, Adi Hastings, and Lisa Heineman—also provided valuable assistance in selecting the panelists for what ended up being an enormously successful series of discussions, whose insights and challenges we hope are reflected in the papers included in this volume. We would also like to thank Sandy Crooms, our editor at The Ohio State University Press, and the three anonymous readers she obtained for our manuscript. Their comments and suggestions were crucial in helping us to select and organize the papers that ended up in this final version of the collection. Finally, we would like to thank our families for putting up with us and our obscenities during the last three years.

PART ONE

Introduction

LOREN GLASS and CHARLES FRANCIS WILLIAMS

Beyond Liberalism?

1857. Gustave Flaubert's *Madame Bovary* and Charles Baudelaire's *Les Fleurs du mal*, inaugural works of literary modernism, are put on trial for offenses against public morals, and the British Parliament passes Lord Campbell's Obscene Publications Act, providing statutory authority for the seizure and destruction of material deemed obscene. Two years later, John Stuart Mill publishes his classic treatise *On Liberty*. We place these events beside each other because they conveniently illustrate the terms within which the category of obscenity would be legislated and debated over the next century, not only in Europe and the United States, but also, thanks to the colonial exportation of Western legal systems, around the globe. On the one hand, we see the modern state acknowledging that artistic expression may pose a threat to traditional morality and taking upon itself the job of adjudicating the nature and extent of that threat. Over the course of the nineteenth century in both Europe and the United States, the state increasingly usurped the traditional authority of the church in regulating and repressing sexual expression and behavior. On the other hand, we see the foundational elaboration of a political theory that identifies that very state function as a threat to individual liberty. And these terms have demographic analogues that further illuminate the struggles to come. Flaubert and Baudelaire mark the inception of a dissident class fragment, an avant-garde community of artists and intellectuals who identified themselves in opposition to the "tyranny of the majority" against which Mill warned. Conversely, the judges who ruled on their cases, and the Parliament that passed Lord Campbell's Act, represent the hegemonic consolidation of what Matthew Arnold called the philistines, the ascendant middle classes that took it upon themselves to regulate and repress the burgeoning electoral majorities represented by increasing working-class literacy and enfranchisement. Obscenity, then, emerges as a marker of division and debate within the consolidating middle-class hegemony of the nation-state era.

It also emerges out of persistent anxieties regarding the status of women within this developing class formation. The first application of Lord Campbell's Act would be *Queen v. Hicklin* (1868), which concerned the sale of a pamphlet entitled "The Confessional Unmasked: shewing the depravity of the Romish priesthood, the iniquity of the Confessional, and the questions put to females in confession." This landmark case established what would become known as the "Hicklin Test": "whether the tendency of the matter charged as obscenity is to deprave and corrupt those whose minds are open to such influences, and into whose hands a publication of this sort may fall."[1] It was widely understood that the "females" in the pamphlet were among "those whose minds are open to such influences," so many Madame Bovarys who might be corrupted by obscene materials which, given rising literacy rates and improved printing technologies, were increasingly available in the bookstalls of London, Paris, and New York. One year later, Mill published *The Subjection of Women,* arguing that "the legal subordination of one sex to the other—is wrong in itself."[2] The long shadow cast by *Hicklin* over the next century would reveal the degree to which obscenity trials were referenda on this threatened tradition of subordination.

Initially, women participated in these trials only as fictional characters or, as in the case of Jane Heap and Margaret Anderson, who serialized *Ulysses* in *The Little Review,* as publishers of modern literature suspected of obscenity. With the notable exception of Radclyffe Hall, who wrote the lesbian classic *The Well of Loneliness,* the authors of obscene literature were men writing about women whose sexual needs and appetites exceeded the protocols of their class. From Emma Bovary to Molly Bloom to Constance Chatterley, the heroines of the modern literature of obscenity are male fantasies of female sexual autonomy. Thus it is far from coincidental that, alongside works of literature, information about contraception and abortion, frequently provided by "family limitation" activists such as Margaret Sanger and Mary Dennett, was also the object of systematic prosecution as obscenity.

The first half of the twentieth century witnessed a gradual and inexorable shift in the terrain of the battle between the philistines and the literati, with the former increasingly ceding ground to the latter. Aesthetic practices and sexual protocols that had previously been the domain of a minority class fraction were increasingly becoming acknowledged and adopted by the burgeoning professional managerial classes, who were inheriting the mantle of moral authority from the genteel middle classes of the Victorian era. And this shift in class hegemony provoked corresponding changes in the cultural marketplace. As representations of, and information about, sexuality became increasingly acceptable to middle-class consumers, the culture industries worked to make such materials more easily available. And, as advertisers began adopting popular psychoanalytic theories equating sexual and consumer desire, it would become increasingly difficult to differentiate between commercial exploitation and aesthetic expression of sexuality.

The distinction was crucial, however, in determining the very different history of censorship in cinema. In the 1915 case of *Mutual Film Corp. v. Industrial Commission of Ohio,* the Supreme Court determined that "the exhibition of moving pictures is a business pure and simple, originated and conducted for profit . . . not to be regarded . . . as part of the press of the country or as organs of public opinion."[3] And this determination would hold until the 1952 case of *Burstyn v. Wilson,* which granted cinema constitutional protections in the United States. The silent era would be marked by scandal and controversy, until Hollywood ultimately decided in 1930 to regulate itself under the provisions of the notorious Production Code. The Code was amended in 1934, and henceforth the depiction of moral issues and sexual practices in American film would be regulated by the stern benevolence of Production Code Chief Joseph Breen and the idiosyncratic exigencies of state film boards. The resulting "long adolescence" of Hollywood film, in which all crimes were punished and even married couples couldn't be shown sleeping in the same bed, provides a potential argument for the productive, as opposed to repressive, powers of censorship.[4]

1957. *Roth v. United States,* followed by the passage of the revised *Obscene Publications Act* in England in 1959, marks a widely acknowledged turning point in the modern history of obscenity. Supreme Court Associate Justice William Brennan updated the test for obscenity as "whether to the average person, applying contemporary community standards, the dominant theme of the material taken as a whole appeals to the prurient interest," and he defined obscenity as speech that is "utterly without redeeming social importance."[5] Although the case affirmed that obscenity would remain an exception to First Amendment protection, this definition had the effect of dramatically narrowing the range of expression that could be included in this exception. This rapidly became evident in the many obscenity trials that followed on the heels of this landmark decision, in which it became increasingly difficult for the courts to identify material with no redeeming value. The authors, critics, publishers, and academics who had successfully institutionalized modern literature from Flaubert to Joyce were now able to liberate the last remaining "underground" classics that had formed a kind of shadow canon to the monuments of modernism.

The "masterpiece" in this canon was D. H. Lawrence's widely banned, and widely pirated, *Lady Chatterley's Lover*, the story of a cross-class romance between an aristocratic woman and her crippled husband's gamekeeper, who liberates her sexually partly through the use of four-letter words. *Lady Chatterley* (the slippage between character and novel was endemic) was put on trial not only in the United States and England, but also in Australia, India, and Japan. The English and American cases were widely heralded as triumphant battles in a war for freedom of expression that appeared, finally, to be won when, in 1968, Lawyer Charles Rembar published *The End of Obscenity*, recounting his successful exoneration in the United States of *Lady Chatterley's Lover*, *Tropic of Cancer*, and *Fanny Hill*. Rembar confidently concluded his book: "So far as writers are concerned, there is no longer a law of obscenity."[6]

A battle had been won, but the war was not over. Indeed, *Lady Chatterley* fared less well in India and Japan. Both trials were deliberated under constitutions based on Anglo-American law, and both courts, making ample use of precedents from English and American trials, found the text to be obscene. And the judges in both cases were aware of the degree to which the liberal framework of Anglo-American law risked obscuring the cultural particularities of the community onto which it had been grafted. On the one hand, Justice Tsuyoshi Mano, concurring with the majority in the Japanese case, nevertheless felt it necessary to mention an ancient Japanese custom called "utagaki," where "a group of young men and women went, hand in hand, up into a mountain, normally regarded as sacred, and there they feasted, sang, and danced; and at the height of pleasure, they engaged openly in indiscriminate group sex acts and indulged in the state of ecstasy." Justice Mano cited this ancient practice in order to "illustrate that a way of thinking like that of the majority opinion which attempts to set up an absolute bound for obscenity irrespective of time and place cannot escape criticism that it is a theory which disregarded clearly established historical facts." Mano buttressed his argument by citing Judge Learned Hand's famous dictum in *United States v. Kennerly* (1913), that obscenity should be determined according to "the present critical point of compromise between candor and shame at which the community may have arrived here and now," but it is nevertheless clear that he is deliberately referencing a tradition whose practice precedes and exceeds modern definitions of obscenity.[7]

If the Japanese case suggests that "ancient customs" may pose a challenge to the liberal framework of modern obscenity law, the Indian case of *Ranjit D. Udeshi v. State of Maharashtra* (1964) reveals a more urgent and contemporary concern. Magistrate J. Hidayatullah, writing for the majority, after detailing the history of Anglo-American obscenity law from Hicklin to Roth, cited the historical specificity of his court's ruling: "Today our national and regional languages are strengthening themselves by new literary standards after a deadening period under the impact of English. Emulation by our writers of an obscene book under the aegis of the Court's determination is likely to pervert our entire literature because obscenity pays and true art finds little popular support." Anticipating contemporary postcolonial theory, Hidayatullah argued that traditionally subordinated populations are not necessarily well served by judicial philosophies that presume formal equality.[8]

Back in the United States, the Supreme Court was attempting to refine and clarify the definition of obscenity that it had established in *Roth*. In *Ginsberg v. New York* (1968), the Court affirmed the constitutionality of New York's Smut Peddling Law, which included a clause specifying "harm to minors" as a legitimate justification for a variable definition of obscenity. Brennan's majority decision established that the state has an "independent interest in the well-being of its youth" that justifies enforcing a lower threshold of legality for sexually explicit materials made available to minors.[9] In the same year, the MPAA would introduce its new ratings system, which replaced the moribund production code with a set of categories designed to codify the difference between minors and adults. The new ratings system also had the somewhat unintended consequence of legitimating the emergent hardcore pornography industry, which quickly appropriated the adults-only "X" rating for its products.

In 1969, Chief Justice Earl Warren retired and the newly elected President Nixon selected the more conservative Warren Burger to replace him. The Burger Court got the opportunity to revisit the seemingly intractable problem of obscenity in the case of *Miller v. CA* (1973). Conceding that "no majority of the Court has at any given time been able to agree on a standard to determine what constitutes obscene, pornographic material," Burger convinced a 5–4 majority to replace the "utterly without redeeming social value" component of its definition with the far lower threshold of "whether the work, taken as a whole, lacks serious literary, artistic, political, or scientific value."[10] Furthermore, conceding that "it is neither realistic nor constitutionally sound to read the First Amendment as requiring that the people of Maine or Mississippi accept public depiction of conduct found tolerable in Las Vegas, or New York City," the majority opinion established that lower courts may use regionally specific community standards in adjudicating cases of obscenity.

Five years later, in the case of *Pacifica v. FCC* (1978), the Supreme Court upheld the FCC's ban on George Carlin's classic monologue "Seven Words You Can't Say on Television," ruling that radio is a "uniquely pervasive" medium and therefore merits a lower threshold of legality regarding purportedly offensive speech.[11] In the *Pacifica* case, the Court affirmed the FCC's definition of "indecency" as speech which does not rise to the level of obscenity but which may be regulated if it is determined that children may hear it. This shift from outright censorship to selective regulation would determine many of the most heated battles of the 1980s and 1990s, as absolute definitions ceded ground to contextual and variable understandings of obscenity and indecency. Correlatively, academic work on sexuality would shift from liberal promotion of sexual freedom and equality to more skeptical considerations of disciplinary discourses in the wake of Michel Foucault's foundational critique of the "repressive hypothesis."[12] In the postmodern era, in other words, liberal theories of freedom increasingly get exposed as feints for actual practices of oppression.

Few figures would epitomize this shift more dramatically than antipornography feminist and legal scholar Catharine MacKinnon, whose work with Andrea Dworkin in the 1970s and 1980s would precipitate a number of ultimately failed attempts to ban hardcore pornography as a violation of the civil rights of women. According to MacKinnon,

> Obscenity law is concerned with morality, specifically morals from the male point of view, meaning the standpoint of male dominance. The feminist critique of pornography is a politics, specifically politics from women's point of view, meaning the standpoint of the subordination

of women to men. Morality here means good and evil; politics means power and powerlessness. Obscenity is a moral idea; pornography is a political practice. Obscenity is abstract; pornography is concrete.[13]

In essence deploying Mill against himself, and echoing Judge Hidayatullah's reasoning above, MacKinnon revealed the possibility that, in the absence of substantive equality, freedom of expression can enable practices of oppression. MacKinnon and Dworkin further turned the tables by focusing on pornography's effects on adult males, extending the long shadow of *Hicklin* into the culture wars of the late twentieth century.

Paralleling the feminist "sex wars," in which MacKinnon and Dworkin would figure so prominently, was the emergence of a generation of radical performance artists who, instead of opposing pornography, in essence reclaimed the bodies it purportedly exploits. Works such as Carolee Schneeman's "Interior Scroll," in which she read from a scroll that she extracted from her vagina, or Annie Sprinkle's "Public Cervix Announcement," in which the audience was invited to view her cervix through a speculum, literally put the artist's body on the line, challenging fundamental distinctions between art and life, expression and conduct. Whether these challenges violated the First Amendment would be put to the test in 1990 when performance artists Karen Finley, Holly Hughes, John Fleck, and Tim Miller, whose contribution to this collection recounts some of these struggles, were denied grants by NEA director John Frohnmeyer, even though they had already been selected through peer review. The so-called "NEA Four" would go on to win their case in court, but the victory was pyrrhic insofar as the NEA, under pressure from conservatives in Congress, ceased funding individual artists. The growing power of neo-conservatism was putting liberals, and liberalism, on the defensive.

At the same time, neoliberal theories of the free market began to trump liberal theories of freedom of expression as the economy increasingly integrated on a global scale. This global neoliberal economy depends on new communications media, and these new media have become crucial in further challenging and confounding liberal protocols for the regulation and even the definition of speech. And if the government has been, for the most part, highly successful in maintaining a powerful outpost of censorship when it comes to traditional broadcast media, it failed miserably when it came to the entirely new media of the Internet. In 1997, the Supreme Court affirmed that the Clinton Administration's *Communications Decency Act,* which was intended to regulate indecency on the Internet, violated the First Amendment. Since then, pornography in all its myriad forms has become an integral, ubiquitous, and highly controversial component of the new media universe.

Recent efforts to regulate Internet pornography have focused almost exclusively on children, once again affirming *Hicklin*'s hold on our sexual mores. Childhood would appear to mark an ultimate limit for liberalism, a stage in the life cycle when the faculties to exercise (or appreciate) freedom of expression are not fully developed. Mill himself affirmed that his "doctrine is meant to apply only to human beings in the maturity of their faculties."[14] As Laura Kipnis's contribution to this collection affirms, adjudicating the sexual and political senses of "maturity" promises to be one of the principal challenges for liberalism in the future.

2007. When we hosted our Obscenity Symposium on the campus of the University of Iowa on March 1–4, we were struck by the contradictory role liberalism played. On the one hand, freedom of expression was the premise and foundation of the event. Without the First Amendment, we probably wouldn't have been able to organize the symposium in the first place. Furthermore, many of the artists and performers we had invited were veterans of the culture wars of the 1980s and 1990s, whose hard won victories had depended on liberalism's fundamental premises. On the other hand, many of the talks interrogated these premises, revealing the degree to which liberalism, which, as we have seen, defined the parameters of the debate over obscenity in the twentieth century, has increasingly been under siege, on the one side from postmodern thinkers skeptical about its andro- and ethnocentric assumptions, and on the other side from religious thinkers doubtful of its moral integrity. Furthermore, this disintegration is occurring in the context of a globalization of culture that increasingly mixes and matches widely different assumptions about the nature of sexuality and the appropriate regulation of its expression. One of the principal challenges for scholars in the twenty-first century will be to formulate new models of research and analysis appropriate to understanding and evaluating obscenity in this new global public sphere. In order to do this, we need to examine it in both its past and its present manifestations. This collection, then, is intended as a casebook that will put recent developments into an historical and global context and chart out possible futures for a debate that clearly promises to persist well into the new millennium.

WE HAVE divided our collection into three sections that are meant to introduce and then elaborate upon the basic terms of this debate. Our introduction is followed by anthropologist Michael Taussig's ruminations on the myriad meanings of obscenity in everyday life. Taussig's meditations reveal both the ubiquity and the ambiguity of obscenity and therefore complement our introduction to the history of its legal regulation. Together, these two introductions present the fundamental definitional challenge that obscenity poses for legal, literary, and anthropological theory.

The two essays in our next section, "The Triumph of Liberalism," illustrate how classical liberalism has addressed this challenge in the United States over the last century. For Nadine Strossen, former President of the ACLU, the impossibility of defining obscenity proves why it should not, and should never have been, an exception to First Amendment protection, and her essay provides both a history and a defense of the ACLU's struggles to eliminate this exception since the landmark passage of *Roth v. United States*. Brett Gary's contribution then provides a prehistory to these struggles in the career of lawyer Morris Ernst, whose successful campaign against censorship in the 1930s established the groundwork for the constitutional debate that would emerge from *Roth*.

Our next, and largest, section, "The Limits of Liberalism," as its title indicates, provides a representative selection of philosophical, methodological, and cultural challenges to liberalism as a framework for debating obscenity. We start off with Tim Miller's performance piece, "Sex/Body/Self," in order to illustrate the ways in which artistic expression has continued to challenge "contemporary community standards" after the so-called end of obscenity. As an example of queer performance art, Miller's piece also illustrates the degree to which the individualist assumptions of classical liberalism cannot always effectively account for the realities of group experience and identification. For this reason, we follow Miller's piece with Jyoti Puri's academic analysis, "Forging Hetero-Collectives," which closely analyzes how forms of collective identity in India are negotiated through obscenity legislation. Puri offers the Foucauldian concept of biopolitics as a tool for understanding and intervening in contemporary struggles over collective identity, which are so central to the legislation of obscenity and artistic expression.

Foucault provides one framework for understanding the limits of liberalism in negotiating the problem of obscenity; Freud provides another. Both Laura Kipnis's discussion of Terry Zwigoff's 1994 biopic about the cartoonist R. Crumb and Mikita Brottman and David Sterritt's meditations on the psychosexual relations between money and feces deploy Freudian theory in order to understand the psychological mechanisms of offense that tend to be obscured by liberal models of the rational individual. More specifically, both of these contributions reveal the degree to which childhood, frequently formulated as a stage during which we should be protected from obscenity, is in fact one of the primary sources of its content.

We conclude with John Peters's "Preludes to a Theory of Obscenity," which argues that, while we cannot trust the agencies of the state to regulate sexual expression, we should nevertheless affirm our opposition to certain forms of that expression in what are essentially moral terms. Noting liberalism's reluctance to hazard moral judgments when it comes to obscenity, Peters suggests that such judgments have been and remain available in the work of a variety of critical thinkers, both ancient and modern, and that these judgments can provide the basis for a more discriminatory engagement with the proliferation of sexual imagery in our contemporary society.

The contrast between Strossen and Peters is clear, and that is why they bookend our collection. However, they both agree in their fundamental opposition to censorship, and this agreement indicates, to us, that liberalism remains essential as a legal framework for negotiating, and protecting, sexual expression in the contemporary world. As a philosophical or psychological theory for understanding the nature and function of that expression, however, liberalism has clearly proven unsatisfactory, and the essays in this volume are intended to offer some alternative methods for achieving this understanding. Ultimately, none of them is able to resolve all the complexities presented by the debate over obscenity, but together they provide the essential coordinates for understanding its political and philosophical stakes.

Notes

1. *Regina v. Hicklin,* 3 Q.B., 360, 362. On the continuing legacy of Hicklin, see Marjorie Heins, *Not in Front of the Children: "Indecency," Censorship, and the Innocence of Youth* (New York: Hill and Wang, 2001).

2. J. S. Mill, *The Subjection of Women,* in Stefan Collini, ed., *On Liberty and Other Writings* (New York: Cambridge University Press, 1989), 119.

3. *Mutual Film Corporation v. Industrial Commission of Ohio,* 236 U.S. 230.

4. On the "long adolescence" of American cinema, see Linda Williams, *Screening Sex* (Durham, NC: Duke University Press, 2008), 25–67.

5. *Roth v. United States,* 354 U.S. 476: 487, 483.

6. Charles Rembar, *The End of Obscenity* (New York: Bantam, 1968), 483.

7. *Judgement upon case of translation and publication of LADY CHATTERLEY'S LOVER and Article 175 of the PENAL CODE*—Supreme Court, 1 March 13, 1957, JPSC, 2.

8. *Ranjit D. Udeshi v. State of Maharashtra* (1964) INSC, 76, 177.

9. *Ginsberg v. New York*, 390 U.S., 629, 630.

10. *Miller v. California*, 413 U.S. 15.

11. *FCC v. Pacifica*, 438 U.S. at 749.

12. Michel Foucault, *The History of Sexuality, Vol. 1: An Introduction*, trans. Robert Hurley (New York: Vintage, 1978), 15–49.

13. Catharine MacKinnon, *Feminism Unmodified: Discourses on Life and Law* (Cambridge, MA: Harvard University Press, 1987), 147.

14. Mill, *On Liberty and Other Writings*, 13.

The Obscene in Everyday Life

JANUARY 1, 2007. My 22-year-old son rents a video from Kim's, titled *Clerks 2*, telling me that *Clerks 1* was pretty funny, and we sit down to watch it around 8:00 at night, the night before he returns to school. He explains that it is a sort of documentary, showing the lives of people who clerk in stores like a 7-Eleven or a McDonald's in New Jersey, a place that to the enlightened people in Manhattan epitomizes obscenity anyway, full of SUVs, suburbs, chemical plants, and people too cheap to live in the city but come to Manhattan weekends to indulge in strip clubs, fancy restaurants, and Broadway shows. Well, after a few minutes we are pretty disgusted; not a single line of dialogue comes out of the mouths of these quintessentially ordinary people in their mid-twenties without reference to genitalia or lurid sexual activity, the movie drawing to a close with a fleshy bald male called Kelly in black leather long johns sucking off a donkey on an improvised stage with a smoke machine in what looks like a McDonald's but for legal reasons, I guess, has an invented name. "It's disgusting," says one of the young women in the movie, referring not to McDonald's but to the size of the donkey's penis off screen, "but I can't stop looking." Georges Bataille could not have put it better with his mantra of attraction and repulsion. Is this the genius of the vernacular? That it can express convoluted highbrow ideas in a pithy phrase enlarged by the *mise-en-scène*? Bataille's other term, made much of by

Julia Kristeva, namely, *the abject*, also springs to mind, a troublesome term that to me suggests a close kinship with the obscene—note the strange prefixes at work here, *ab*ject and *ob*scene, and start to plot your etymologies. This movie, I say to myself, must be a particularly revealing instance of so-called popular culture, which I always feel I am missing out on and don't really know what it is. Once you have bracketed it like that and given it a name, "popular culture," I fear you have already lost it. Could the same apply to the obscene? Thank God I have this son of mine who knows popular culture inside out and when home from school acts as my guide, as did the pagan Virgil to Dante, lost and confused, making his way ever deeper underground to the nether parts of the devil himself on his way to redemption. They say it's adults who educate children, but nowadays it's so obviously the other way around, at least when it comes to popular culture. When I was a kid in Australia in 1952, I went to see a locally made movie called *Bush Christmas* in which two friends of mine from up the road, Nicky Yardley and his brother Michael, starred. What a thrill it was to see the credits flash on and then the sign, "Adults Only Permitted if Accompanied by Children." The film concerned a handful of children, boys and girls, outwitting some bushrangers. How crazily innocent it all seems when viewed from today with movies like *Clerks 2*! What has happened in the intervening years, along with everyday reports of child abuse, hysteria about so-called sex offenders stigmatized as loathsome beasts, and pre-pubescent girls acting like sex kittens, as depicted poignantly toward the end of the wonderful movie *Little Miss Sunshine*? Which of these categories of behavior deserve to be called *obscene* and which do not? This question is made all the more complex by the fact that in *Clerks 2* the obscenities—if that's a fair epithet—are so terribly natural, unstressed, unexcited and unexciting, like someone asking for a Big Mac or a Coke, in which case, why bother? Why the autistic lack of emotion about the obscene? Is this the new sitcom, sex without sex? Could this be the ultimate sanitization of society, de-eroticizing the erotic?

JANUARY 2. Downtown Manhattan in a bar waiting for my other son. I am thinking of writing something about obscenity and am pondering how much the Western world has changed with respect to the moving line separating the obscene from the non-obscene. When Thomas Hardy got his most celebrated novel, *Jude the Obscure*, published in England just over one hundred years ago, it was greeted with shock at the attack on marriage, class, and sexual mores, meriting a review entitled

Jude the Obscene. In *Sister of the Road: The Autobiography of Boxcar Bertha,* by the anarchist obstetrician-gynecologist and lover of Emma Goldman, Ben Reitman, Bertha tells us of her beloved mother's father, a farmer in Kansas who, in the 1880s, was one of the organizers of the free-love convention at Worcester, Massachusetts. This man served three terms in jail, two of which were for sending birth control information through the mail, which the federal authorities called obscene. And as regards this moving line separating the obscene from the non-obscene, isn't it a curious fact that I find it difficult, if not impossible, to define one or the other of these terms outside of their coupling as mutually antago-nistic opposites, the same way as Émile Durkheim defines the sacred, as not the profane? I am early, so I sit by the bar after locking my bike outside on Sixth Avenue, where I notice a bearded muscle-bound guy in his forties dressed in black looking like Kelly from the movie last night sitting outside on this cold early evening by a lonely table smok-ing a cigarette and talking avidly into the cell phone cradled in his ear. A far cry from the haunts of the bridge-and-tunnel crowd from New Jersey, the bar has yet to fill up with its usual crowd of yuppie bohemi-ans and academics like myself. A man and woman are sort of making out, seated at a table by the window, looking pretty glum. Three or four guys are at the bar talking chummily with the barman. A cute young waitress tying on her apron takes my order and over a glass of red wine balanced on a tiny copper-topped table I try to read my novel, *Distant Star* by the Chilean Roberto Bolano "the most influential and admired novelist in the Spanish-speaking world," according to Susan Sontag. I notice a camouflage-patterned backpack hanging over the chair next to me. Immersed in the mysteries of the strange poet—or is he a spy?—in the time when Pinochet took power in Chile, I fail to notice the entry of the bearded muscle man from outside, sans cigarette, who, despite there being plenty of empty seats, sits down right beside me speaking loudly in an Oh! I am so Gay! manner of speech into his cell phone, so loudly and with such flair that you had to wonder if actually he wasn't talking primarily to the few people in the bar for whom the supposed person at the other end of the phone was merely an excuse. "So we went to the hospital," he booms, "and she's gonna have . . ."—and he opens a note book and slowly reads out, syllable by syllable, "palliative treatment." "This is good," he goes on to say in a voice at once cajoling and authoritative, a voice that brooks no dissent, as he describes what happened yesterday, what happened today with the lung tissue slides at Sloan Kettering, and how all of that connects with what will happen tomorrow with the ambulance to White Plains. I am sitting there like an idiot unable to shut out this saga. It seems like the other person on the phone never speaks, pulverized by this monologue and perhaps by grief and anxiety. It is sickening to be exposed to this intimacy, the intimacy of death, no matter how anonymous such dying might be with respect to the captive audience in the bar, and I have little hesitation, although I do have some, in designating this activity as obscene. The hesitation I have has to do with the way people often refer to something they dislike as "obscene," thus injecting moral condemnation where it doesn't seem to quite fit. This is puzzling to me, and its delineation might shed light on the meaning, today, of obscenity. To offer what might not be the best example of what I have in mind here, let me recall a strange moment in a collapsing Anthropology Department full of rancor. A first-year graduate student was giving a talk, accompanied by slides, on the eating clubs at Princeton where he had been a student, his talk being billed as one of those rare occasions where the secrets, or should I say sociology, of the rich and privileged are to be revealed. This was according to the senior professor, whose disgust at the rich and powerful was equaled only by her desire to become one of them. Her protégé, an untenured professor of similar disposition, chimed in when, trying to deal with the problem of whether it was ethical to show the faces of the Princeton students photographed, someone proposed that maybe the faces could be masked in some way or blurred. "That would be truly obscene," he thundered, a statement I remember vividly as if it was yesterday, even though it occurred some twelve years ago. Turning this over in my mind, as has been my wont at unexpected moments over the years, I keep wondering why this would be thought of as obscene, indeed "truly obscene," and frankly I have no answer. What I do feel sure about is that all of us in that room were with that remark being marshaled like sheep to pass into a scary place where one was to be morally strip-searched, and, worst of all, we had no idea what we had done wrong. In other words, it was not the suggestion about masking and making persons anonymous that was obscene, "truly obscene," but that rejoinder itself, suggesting that those who would designate something as obscene are playing with fire and may well turn out to be far more obscene than what they rail against. The line dividing the obscene from the non-obscene is anything but clear, anything but stable, and, what is more, is such that even to name it, even to mark it, is to run the risk of adding to obscenity's mysterious power and fall victim to its stigmatizing effluvium. But enough of this madness and back to the bar on Sixth Ave where, having finally laid his phone to rest, the bearded man, obviously a favored customer, perhaps a waiter himself or even the manager, calls over one of the young men waiting tables the second he has disposed of his phone and in an even louder voice than before says, "Hi Mark, you're the worst sex I've ever had in my life." Not even Bataille with his marked interest in the confluence of sex and death could have predicted the perfection with which his theory would manifest itself as it did that second day of the New Year, 2007. I pack my bag and take Roberto Bolano's *Distant Star* over to a table as far away as possible in the back room aglow with Christmas lights.

JANUARY 3. Now that I've got this idea of an "obscenity diary" I am training myself to be more conscious of obscenity and am wondering why this so interests me. I am now in a more activist mode, fine-tuning my antennae to the obscene instead of just waiting passively for it to happen. Three years back my friend Jimmie Durham sent me a copy of his nature journal that he kept for many months in Berlin and I thought it wonderful, matter-of-fact whimsy concerning the odd bird that makes its appearance towards the end of winter, some new grass by the canal, the character of the frost. What made it charming was the basic idea that nature in the city is a fascinating topic, like an illegal immigrant hiding out between the artificial splendor of the well-ordered parks on one side, and car exhaust on the other. But it is the cast of mind that's important here—not so much what one is looking for, but the way one looks—as when Jimmie writes his entry for December 24, 2000, about buying a wild goose, cooking it, then the first snow of the year falls around five in the evening, everything becomes white and quiet and he goes out onto the small terrace and hears a crow calling in the distance. This sense of nature as antithetical to the city, as a wild intruder lurking in the background waiting its time, is surely analogous to obscenity with its necessary affinities to what is deemed right and proper, reminding me of the story I was told by my British anthropologist friend Olivia Harris in the 1970s of how surprised everyone was when the British government built one of its first motorways, the M1, and instead of fleeing, the rabbits returned to the edges of the motorway and built their burrows right there, apparently enjoying the vibrations. Is that rabbit analogous to obscenity? Once conscious of my new mission I start seeing obscenity everywhere. In the swimming pool today there is this really fat man who looks so obscene in the shower with his tummy falling over his thighs and black hair over his back. Swimming he looks like a whale having a seizure. But now you have to be careful because fatness is not a laughing matter, what with juvenile diabetes, largely caused by fast food joints such as the one in *Clerks 2,* and fatness has been dignified as a Civil Right. McDonald's breathes a little easier. And anyway, aren't we each and all free agents, responsible for how we look and what we eat? I ask myself, what would Jimmie's diary have to say about this nature in the city? Leaving the pool, I get on my daughter's vintage Schwinn bike and pedal through Central Park. It is a fine day. People are happy. In fact it is too damn fine, almost a summer day and it is the middle of winter. The radio tells me that 2007 will be the hottest year ever. The planet is in trouble. My dentist chuckles over my gaping mouth. She has a sunny disposition and can be very funny, an advantage, I would think, for someone who has to look down into smelly, cavity-riddled mouths and wobbling tonsils all the time such that it becomes just another boring day at the office. Well, maybe not quite, which is where a TV program like *MASH* gets its humor, mixing the sacred opening of the human body by scalpels and retractors with the routines of the operating theater, same as William Burroughs's famous "routines," he called them in his letters to Allen Ginsberg, concerning Doctor Benway throwing scalpels and swabs around in gay abandon. Not quite so funny are my memories of medical school, of the year we students spent in small teams of four or five dissecting the human corpse, one team at the top, head and trunk, the other team below that when, to my horror, I was told by a friend that one of our fellow students, a star athlete, was cutting out part of the female genitalia from several corpses and keeping them in a match box. We are used in anthropology to the concept of "licensed transgression," those occasions societies set aside, such as initiation rites or Saturday nights, when the rules of decorum are relaxed or transgressed, by permission, as it were, thus making of transgression a complicated business indeed, partly rule breaking, partly rule conserving. In such a situation is obscenity truly obscenity, and what then of unlicensed transgression, as with the scalpel wielding medical student whom none of us informed on? "Well," my dentist says, probing tooth Number Eighteen, "we ruined this one [meaning the planet Earth], let's move on to the next!" "And everyone laughing and enjoying the lovely warm sunlit end of the world," I say between opening and closing my mouth. And she laughs too. When I rode though the park, black nannies in droves were pushing white babies in baby carriages under the pines that the wealthy people on the Upper East Side have donated. A black man sat playing a drum with a small coat on the ground for coins. He was still there two and half hours later when I pedaled home, playing the tom-tom for the white folks. Opposite the Metropolitan Museum of Art a mammoth stretch limo black and shiny suddenly pulls out. Could have killed me. Parks illegally and is still there when I pedal back hours later, motor running the full complement of carbon monoxide, the driver barely visible behind the dark glass of the window in his suit and tie peering into a small computer as his hedge fund boss does deals with the museum. Does anyone really know what a "hedge fund" is, by the way? And they say magic has been driven out of the world. Thinking about the history of the Louvre, in one of his more memorable Surrealist pieces for his famous dictionary in his 1930 magazine, *Documents,* Georges Bataille stated that the art gallery in our time has taken over as the sacred site in the center of the city that was the king's palace. The story goes like this: When the king was beheaded in public view during the French Revolution—there in the center of the city where the Egyptian Obelisk was a few years later placed by Napoleon— at the same time as he lost his head, so the city's abattoir, also in the heart of the city, alive with blood and offal, was moved to anonymous locations outside of the city and people could then enjoy their Sundays of purification by going to the art gallery while the obscene roots of the sacred such as sacrifice of the god or animals is nowhere in evidence. That was written almost eighty years ago, and while the general idea is as relevant and as riveting as ever, there are other sacred, or should one say *negatively sacred,* sites that undergo the same disappearance as Bataille's abattoir. I am told for instance by a mechanic friend in upstate New York that none of the towns in the vicinity allow junk yards, which he calls *salvage* yards, to be exposed to the public, and they have to be situated outside of the towns. The county town planner and the town clerk both inform me that local laws demand high walls around such yards, which must be on the outskirts, never inside, the town, and the same applies to strip joints, which are not allowed to have blue lighting on the outside. In town planning parlance strip clubs are called "adult uses" and fall into the more general category of LULUS, meaning Local Unwanted Land Uses, which includes slaughterhouses as well. No prime space on Fifth Avenue like the Met for them! No wonder that a Mom in Texas got confused recently when her ten-year-old was taken on a public-school outing to the art gallery in Dallas and came home talking of statues of naked women and as a result the art teacher was fired. What are naked ladies doing in the center of town? The town of Rosendale near where I live upstate, a town with a population of roughly 5,000, two hours north of New York City, had a plan drawn up by a Republican councilman and chief of the Fire District a few years back for an industrial zone—"park," I think they called it—which would destroy many beautiful acres of what remains of the forest by the river, and this, he added earnestly, would be just perfect for "adult uses" as well. So is this the new sacred geography of America, walled off junk—I mean salvage—yards with gutted motor vehicles alongside windowless sex clubs—I mean "adult uses"—with low ceilings and dark lighting forming along with the slaughterhouses a ring of outposts around the perimeter of what passes for a town center of gas stations, churches, and convenience stores selling lottery tickets? As I cycle back through the park the sun is setting and it is getting nippy. The black nannies are wrapping up their charges and heading home. Some tourists are taking photos of the sun visible through the spaces left by the skyscrapers to the south as foregrounded by the trees of the park. The contrast is overwhelming. This is the New York sublime, better than the Grand Canyon. In front of me on a beat-up dirt bike an elderly man, Hispanic and poor looking, is leisurely cycling, hunched over the handlebars. From somewhere invisible on his person or his bike enchanting music is pouring out real loud. I mean *really* loud. It sounds like Coltrane and in this setting it is beyond all expectation and stereotype, which is why, I think, the gaggle of uncomforted looking Upper East side folk sitting on the benches admiring the sunset, find this obscene, yet sacred too, and don't know what to do.

JANUARY 4, 2007. Many years ago as Europe took the first steps toward the Holocaust, Bataille's colleague Michel Leiris gave a blessedly short talk to the College of Sociology in Paris as his contribution to what his Surrealist colleagues were calling "sacred sociology." He called the talk "The Sacred in Everyday Life," and after running through memories of his childhood, such as the mysterious yet familiar glow of the stove, *La Radieuse,* in the kitchen, his father's silver plated revolver, secretive bathroom antics with his brother, and children's games with language, Leiris concluded that the sacred was not restricted to formal situations such as the rituals of the church but existed as a living force in everyday life, the mark of which was danger, ambiguity, mystery, and the unexpected surprise or shock we might associate with the Surreal. This account differs remarkably from the notion of the sacred set forth in 1912 by Émile Durkheim in his famous work *The Elementary Forms of the Religious Life,* in which the sacred was designated as a feeling of awe, reverence, and fear associated with something set firmly apart from the everyday, which he designated as the profane, a confusing word that means both mundane or ordinary as well as the negative sacred. Leiris challenged—or seemed to challenge—this distinction between sacred and profane by locating the sacred in the profane, granting the sacred a light and play-ful character, but Bataille went further in emphasizing the obscene basis of the sacred, no less than the sacred basis of the obscene. Little more than an inversion of Leiris's sacred in everyday life, my obscenity diary displays, I believe, something important to this montage-effect of purity coexisting side by side with impurity by having them run one after the other in daisy chains of uneven yet daily occurrence that tear at our logic no less than our language. As regards my diary approach, Witt-genstein does this too. He talks about our talk and wonders out loud about our apparent confusions and contradictions but most of all about our senselessness—of which we are blissfully unaware— especially when we adopt the high road of the meta-level and ask unanswerable ques-tions such as What is the Sacred or What is obscene? Leiris spotted this dilemma too—for dilemma it surely is—as these questions are as impor-tant as they are unanswerable. In my hubris I have extended Wittgen-stein and Leiris by writing little scenes or ethnographic sketches with each one serving as a comment on the one preceding, searching for a language that can perhaps do justice to the unsayable no less than the unsaid.

PART TWO

The Triumph of Liberalism

Defending the F-Word

Freedom![1]

Our legal system has always treated sexual expression with singular hostility, relegating it to second-class status under the First Amendment. This discriminatory treatment reflects a broader cultural pattern, which was well captured by Susan Sontag when she wrote, "Since Christianity . . . concentrated on sexual behavior as the root of virtue, everything pertaining to sex has been a 'special case' in our culture, evoking peculiarly inconsistent attitudes."[2] Accordingly, to borrow again from Sontag, "expression pertaining to sex has been a special case in our law, evoking peculiarly inconsistent rulings."

The First Amendment's Free Speech Clause is written in unqualified language, barring any "law . . . abridging the freedom of speech."[3] It makes no exception for speech about sex. However, the Supreme Court has consistently read such an exception into the First Amendment. It has allowed sexual speech to be restricted or even banned under circumstances in which it would not allow other types of speech to be limited.[4]

Overall, American law is the most speech-protective in the world. The U.S. legal system protects many kinds of speech that are widely considered offensive or dangerous, including those that are outlawed in other advanced democracies, such as hate speech,[5] defamatory falsehoods about government officials,[6] and the advocacy of violence and lawbreaking.[7] In contrast, American law singles out for suppression sexual expression, a type of speech that *is* protected under many other legal systems.[8]

As an activist, I am congenitally an optimist, so I want to stress that there have been some positive legal developments in this area in recent years, and there are also important ongoing law reform initiatives, led by the ACLU, along with many diverse allies. I will save the details of that upbeat assessment of future trends for later, so I can end on a positive note! Before then, I will address three other major points. First, I will cite some examples of our legal system's ongoing assault on sexual expression. Second, I will outline the general free-speech principles that strongly protect expression with any other content (other than sexual) to highlight the discriminatory double standard for sexual expression. Third, I will summarize the three major speech-suppressive doctrines that the Supreme Court has concocted to rationalize three major types of restrictions on sexual expression. And then, fourth and finally, I will explain the positive constitutional law developments to which I referred above.

I. Our legal system's ongoing assault on sexual expression

Starting in 2004, we saw dramatic new crackdowns on "indecency" in broadcasts in response to the now infamous "wardrobe malfunction"[9] during the televised 2004 Super Bowl halftime show.[10] These new measures are so extreme that they even have been condemned by some former officials of the Federal Communications Commission (the "FCC") itself, even though these officials had supported prior FCC limits on broadcast indecency.[11] Yet even these former policemen of the airwaves felt compelled to denounce the recent repression as "a radical . . . censorship crusade that will . . . chill . . . all but the blandest . . . program fare."

Since the Super Bowl brouhaha in 2004—which one journalist memorably called "a tempest in a B-cup"[12]—the FCC has imposed record-breaking fines on broadcasters, even for the fleeting, spontaneous use of a single word in a clearly non-sexual context. For example, the FCC condemned a documentary film about blues musicians, which was produced by Martin Scorsese and broadcast by an educational television station, because one or more of the artists being interviewed uttered what the FCC coyly calls "the F-word" or "the S-word."[13] The FCC even ruled that the news program *The Early Show* had committed "indecency" through one use of the word "bullshitter"; the FCC stressed that its censorial regime contains "no . . . exemption [for news]."[14]

As if all of the FCC censorship has not been bad enough, in 2005 Congress passed a repressive new federal law that vastly increases the fines for broadcast indecency—by a factor of 10.[15] Under this new Broadcast Decency Enforcement Act, the use of one four-letter word, even in a clearly non-sexual context, can trigger a fine of $325,000. Small, nonprofit broadcasters would be bankrupted by such huge fines. Therefore, to avoid them, many broadcasters have pulled many valuable programs.[16] For example, a PBS station cancelled a historical documentary about Marie Antoinette because it contained sexually suggestive drawings.[17] Likewise, CBS affiliates pulled a documentary about the 9/11 terrorist attacks just because it included actual footage of shocked onlookers watching the Twin Towers crashing down.[18] Not surprisingly, many of them were exclaiming in horror, but the documentary never aired because some of the horrified exclamations included four-letter words. Given the government's zero-tolerance policy toward isolated expletives, a Vermont public radio station even barred a United States Senate candidate from a political debate.[19] The station manager feared that the candidate might do on air what he had done during a previous live debate; he had lost his temper and called two audience members "shits."[20]

The recent attacks on sexual expression have not been limited to broadcasting. For example, the federal law suppressing online material that any local community deems "harmful to minors," which the ACLU had fought for more than a decade, concluded its circuitous journey through the federal court system in 2009 and was finally pronounced dead under the First Amendment. This law was the badly misnamed the Child Online Protection Act or COPA.[21] It was "badly misnamed" because, far from protecting children, it potentially criminalized any online expression that contained any sexual content, ranging from Planned Parenthood's information about contraception to artistic websites that display nude paintings or sculptures. Both the lower court and the intermediate appellate court ruled that the law was unconstitutionally overbroad and vague, outlawing significant expression that the First Amendment clearly protects.[22] Even the trial judge in that case noted that blocking young people's access to such material may well do them more harm than good.[23] I stress that *even* this judge took this position because he is a conservative Republican, who was appointed by a conservative Republican president,[24] as was the judge who wrote the intermediate appellate court opinion affirming the trial judge's ruling.[25]

These facts illustrate an important point that contravenes common stereotypes. When it comes to freedom of speech, including for sexual expression, both support and opposition cut across all party and ideological lines.[26] That is one reason the ACLU always has been staunchly non-partisan, never supporting or opposing any official or candidate, but instead praising or criticizing them on an issue-by-issue basis.[27] All politicians are positive on some civil liberties issues and negative on others. When it comes to sexual expression, the major division is not between Democrats and Republicans or between liberals and conservatives. Rather, the major division lies between, on the one hand, elected officials and, on the other hand, officials who are relatively sheltered from the political process and its majoritarian pressures: federal judges.

This pattern is illustrated by the recent censorial laws and regulations I noted above. In 2006, the new federal law that cracks down on broadcast "indecency" was passed by overwhelming margins in both houses of Congress.[28] In fact, *not a single* Senator voted against it, while in the House, only 35 brave souls voted no. Likewise, all five members of the FCC strongly supported that censorial new law, as well as the recent record-breaking fines on broadcasters.[29] In contrast, though, just as elected officials and their FCC appointees have supported broadcast censorship across the political spectrum, the opposite is true of federal judges. Fortunately, federal judges have opposed such censorship across the political spectrum.[30]

The same pattern has emerged in decisions regarding censorship of online sexual expression. In recent years, Congress passed two such cybercensorship laws,[31] with almost no opposing votes on either side of the aisle.[32] Former presidents Bill Clinton and George W. Bush both defended these laws in the courts against the ACLU's constitutional challenges. In contrast, of the dozens of federal judges who ruled on these cybercensorship laws, almost every single one ruled in the ACLU's favor, voting to uphold freedom of online sexual expression and striking down these repressive laws.

Other recent assaults on sexual expression have occurred outside the legislature and courtroom and have slipped largely below the public radar screen. For example, President Bush's first Attorney General, John Ashcroft, was well-known for his commitment to eradicating sexually oriented expression from our lives, even going so far as to spend $8,000 of our tax dollars to buy drapes to cover an artistically acclaimed Art Deco statue in the Justice Department's main hall just because this toga-clad female figure had one exposed breast![33]

Most people are unaware that Ashcroft's successor, Alberto Gonzales, outdid his predecessor in targeting sexual expression. After Gonzales became Attorney General in 2005, he announced in his very first major public address that the Justice Department would step up its enforcement efforts against such expression.[34] Gonzales told the National Press Club that he was creating a top-flight obscenity prosecution task force, which "will be staffed with our best and brightest."[35] Notably, this move drew widespread criticism from Justice Department lawyers[36] and law enforcement officers,[37] who resented the reallocation of personnel and other resources from other areas that they considered more urgent than preventing consenting adults from viewing images of other consenting adults. One such critic, the U.S. Attorney in Miami, was forced by Gonzales' new initiative to remove agents from child endangerment cases, in which actual children had been physically abused, to reallocate these agents to cases involving sexual images produced by and for adults.[38] As one FBI agent said, "I guess this means we've won the war on terror. We must not need any more resources for espionage."[39] In the same vein, a leader of the American Bar Association said, "Compared to terrorism, public corruption, and narcotics, [pornography] is no worse than dropping gum on the sidewalk."[40]

U.S. Attorneys who aggressively pursued obscenity cases (even those that were quickly thrown out of court) were promoted within the Bush Justice Department, while at least two U.S. Attorneys were reprimanded and even fired because they did not want to deploy their limited resources to fight obscenity cases. A U.S. Attorney from Nevada was pressured to pursue an obscenity case he described as "woefully deficient"; he did not want to reassign to it prosecutors who were working on public corruption and violent crime cases, and he was ultimately fired after resisting Bush Administration demands.[41]

Prime targets of Gonzales's renewed War on Obscenity were images of bondage and sado-masochistic sex.[42] That provoked a commentator on Salon.com to observe, "Many Americans would likely find such pornography appalling. But shouldn't they be far more appalled by the fact that the man now focused on eradicating staged acts of torture was the same one who set the stage, as Bush's counsel, for real acts of torture at Abu Ghraib prison in Iraq?"[43]

While there have been no publicized federal examples of such censorial behavior since the Obama Administration took office, state officials continue to engage in similar acts of sexual censorship. In 2010, when Bob McDonnell became Governor of Virginia, his Attorney General ordered new lapel pins of the state's official seal for his staff because he believed the woman depicted on the seal should have "more modest attire." The original state seal, which since 1776 had pictured the Roman Goddess Virtus with her left breast exposed, was replaced with a new rendition that covered the breast with an armored plate.[44]

II. General free-speech principles that strongly protect expression with non-sexual content should be extended to sexual speech

The starting point for understanding freedom of speech is, of course, the "Free Speech Clause" of the First Amendment to the U.S. Constitution.[45] In sweeping, unqualified terms, it declares that the government "shall make no law abridging the freedom of speech." It does not limit that guarantee to speech about certain topics. In fact, it does not recognize any exceptions at all. In this sense, our constitutional right to free speech is strikingly different from the counterpart provisions in other countries' constitutions.[46] These other constitutions *do* expressly limit free speech in certain circumstances, including for the promotion of public morals,[47] yet our First Amendment framers deliberately rejected such limiting language.

Conservative judges and politicians often stress that the Constitution should be interpreted according to its plain language and original intent.[48] They accuse liberal judges of being "activists" by reading additional meanings into the Constitution's own terms or by departing from the intent that those terms reveal.[49] But in relation to the Free Speech Clause, the judicial activists are all the judges who have read into its straightforward language various unwritten limits, even though the framers deliberately chose *not* to include any. And the "activist" judges who have rewritten the Free Speech Clause in this way include many conservatives.[50] It bears repeating that support for free speech crosses ideological and party lines. However, the same is true of opposition to free speech. Almost everyone advocates reading *some* limits into the Free Speech Clause, for the expression of whatever ideas *they* personally consider offensive, evil, or otherwise inconsistent with their own deeply held beliefs. Journalist Nat Hentoff well captured this pattern in the title of one of his books: *Freedom of Speech for ME, but not for THEE; How the Left and Right Relentlessly Censor Each Other.*[51] A writer for the *Los Angeles Times* also summarized this idea very well when he wrote, "The urge to censor is the most fundamental human drive—far more basic than the sex drive."

At the heart of the Supreme Court's extensive free-speech rulings are two key principles. The first of these principles specifies what is *not* a sufficient justification for restricting speech, and the second prescribes what is a sufficient justification. These principles have been widely accepted by Justices across the ideological spectrum, and they have well served both individual liberty and our democratic society. There is no justification for not extending them to sexual expression, as many judges and scholars have advocated.

The first of these basic principles requires "content neutrality" or "viewpoint neutrality." In essence, the government may never limit speech just because the viewpoint it conveys is considered offensive or otherwise negative by any person or group, even if such group consists of the vast majority of the community.[52] Consistent with this core principle, the Court has protected speech that conveys ideas that are deeply offensive to most Americans, including burning an American flag[53] or burning a cross.[54] The content-neutrality principle reflects the philosophy that the appropriate response to speech that you find offensive or negative in any way is not censorship, but rather either ignoring it or answering back. The Supreme Court described that first option in a recent case that, notably, rejected restrictions on sexual expression on cable TV. The Court said, "Where the [intended] benefit of a content-based speech restriction is to shield the sensibilities of listeners, the . . . right of expression prevails. . . . We are expected to protect our own sensibilities simply by averting [our] eyes."[55]

In contrast, the second general principle of speech regulation states that the government *may* regulate speech if the regulation is necessary to promote some extremely important goal, such as preventing imminent physical harm.[56] This can be illustrated through the flag-burning example. If a protestor is burning a flag in a place where it causes an imminent danger of spreading the fire, then the government may stop that particular flag burning. This principle is often summarized by saying that the government may limit speech that poses "a clear and present danger"[57] of some tangible harm. But speech still may *not* be restricted because of some more remote or speculative harm. In other words, government may not restrict speech on the ground that it (i) *might* cause or lead to some (ii) *intangible* harm, such as offended feelings.[58]

Let me explain each of those two key limits on the government's power to regulate speech. First, if we allowed speech to be curtailed on the speculative basis that it *might* indirectly lead to some possible harm, free speech as we know it would cease to exist. That is because *all* speech *might* lead to potential danger sometime in the future. Justice Oliver Wendell Holmes recognized this fact when he observed that "[e]very idea is an incitement."[59] If we banned all ideas that might lead individuals to actions that might have an adverse impact on important concerns, such as safety, then scarcely any idea would be safe, and surely no idea would be safe that challenged the status quo. This point was stressed by a respected conservative federal Judge, Frank Easterbrook, in an important opinion that struck down a law seeking to punish certain sexual expression that many people consider offensive and that many believe has the potential to cause serious harm at some future time.[60]

Specifically, some advocates of women's rights have sought to ban certain sexual expression on the ground that it degrades or demeans women; hence, they believe that this "pornography," as they call it, endangers women's safety and equality.[61] The City of Indianapolis passed a law reflecting this belief in 1984.[62] The Indianapolis law defined illegal "pornography" as sexually oriented expression that "subordinates" women. It was immediately challenged by First Amendment advocates and advocates of women's rights.[63] Notably, the law's opponents—including Yours Truly—believed not only that it would violate the fundamental free-speech principles that I have been discussing, but also that it would do more harm than good for women. The law even suppressed sexually oriented expression that is essential for women's rights, such as expression about women's sexual and reproductive health. Every judge who ruled on the law agreed that it did violate the core free-speech principles at stake.[64]

In the most extended opinion, Judge Easterbrook assumed for the sake of argument that the law's proponents correctly believed that "depictions of subordination [may] perpetuate subordination." However, he explained that if this were enough to justify suppressing speech, then there would be no free speech left because so much speech has the same potential negative influence. As he wrote:

> Efforts to suppress communist speech in the U.S. were based on the belief that [it] would increase the likelihood of totalitarian government. . . . The [1798] Alien and Sedition Acts . . . rested on a sincerely held belief that disrespect for the government leads to social collapse and revolution—a belief with support in the history of many nations. Racial bigotry, anti-Semitism, violence on television, reporters' biases— these and many more influence the culture and shape our socialization. . . . Yet all is protected as speech, however insidious. Any other

answer leaves the government in control . . . the great . . . director of which thoughts are good for us.[65]

Now I will briefly explain why government may not suppress speech based on intangible harms such as hurt feelings. First, it is important to note that the cardinal free-speech rule that Judge Easterbrook laid out does not at all reflect disrespect for the seriousness of these psychic or emotional harms. Contrary to the old nursery rhyme "Sticks and stones may break my bones but words will never hurt me," words *do* wound, especially when they insult some core element of our identities, such as race, gender, sexual orientation, and so forth. The reason we do not let government suppress speech to prevent these very real psychic or emotional harms is well summed up by another old saying, "The cure is worse than the disease." Hearing offensive and upsetting expression is the lesser of two evils for both society as a whole and individuals. Far worse would be empowering the government, or a majority of our fellow citizens, to take away our individual freedom to make our own choices about what we say and what we see or hear.

To highlight the second-class status to which sexual speech has been relegated under the First Amendment, we can look at just one of the Supreme Court's many cases that abide by the two general speech-protective principles I have just summarized. The Court consistently protects non-sexual expression no matter how offensive and upsetting it is to those who are exposed to it. If these same speech-protective principles were applied to sexual expression, the Supreme Court would strike down anti-obscenity laws, as well as restrictions on broadcast indecency, instead of upholding these suppressive measures as it has done in the past.

Cohen v. California,[66] decided in 1971, is possibly the Court's most important precedent concerning constitutional protection for offensive speech in general—that is, non-sexual offensive speech. The *Cohen* Court held that the F-word in the title of this essay—"Freedom"— extends to what the FCC means by the "F-word"—the one with four letters. So the FCC's recent crackdown on that F-word, in broadcasts, is completely contrary to the *Cohen* case. The FCC crackdown, as well as the new federal statute censoring broadcast "indecency," rests on the very debatable view that speech should receive less protection when it is conveyed by the broadcast media than when it is conveyed by other media. This view goes back to the Supreme Court's ruling in a controversial 1978 case involving Pacifica Radio.[67] I will say a bit more about that case in the next section of this essay. In this section, though, I will continue to discuss the 1971 *Cohen* case, which I think should govern all expression, including sexual expression, in all media, including broadcast.

The *Cohen* case arose during the Vietnam War and upheld Paul Cohen's First Amendment right to wear a jacket, inside a courthouse, on which he had written a message that was very offensive to many people, not only because it contained the four-letter F-word, but also because of his larger message. Specifically, Paul Cohen's jacket proclaimed: "Fuck the draft." The majority opinion that upheld Paul Cohen's right to display this provocative message was written by the much-respected Justice John Marshall Harlan. Notably, Harlan was a conservative Republican, who had been appointed by a Republican president.[68] I stress these facts again to underscore the key point I made earlier: strong support for freedom of speech cuts across party and ideological lines.

Many conservatives want to limit government power over our private lives, leaving decisions about what we say, what we see and hear, and what our own young children see and hear, up to us, instead of letting the government dictate these choices for us. This free-speech approach is not only consistent with individual liberty; it also benefits society as a whole because it permits the lively exchange of ideas and free flow of information that improve democratic decision-making.

Justice Harlan's opinion for the Court in the *Cohen* case well captures both of these essential benefits of protecting offensive expression, the benefits to individual and society alike:

> The . . . right of free expression . . . is designed to remove governmental restraints from . . . public discussion, putting the decision as to what views shall be voiced largely into the hands of each of us, in the hope that . . . such freedom will ultimately produce a more capable citizenry and more perfect polity and in the belief that no other approach would comport with the . . . individual dignity and choice upon which our political system rests.[69]

In essence, to quote another old saying: different strokes for different folks. In our wonderfully diverse society we all have widely divergent ideas, values, and tastes concerning what expression is offensive and what is not. Therefore, if we allowed government to regulate or punish any speech that any person or group considered offensive, we would have little speech left. As the *Cohen* Court put it, "One [person's] vulgarity is another [person's] lyric."[70]

I once saw a cartoon that captures this point. It shows three people in an art museum looking at a classic nude female torso, a fragment of an ancient sculpture minus limbs. Each viewer's reaction is shown in an air bubble. The first one thinks, "Art!" The second thinks, "SMUT!" The third thinks, "An insult to amputees!"

Sexuality is an especially personal area; our views about it are even more subjective than in other areas. Thus, the government is especially wrong to take away our individual right to choose concerning sexual expression. We cannot delegate to any government official—or anyone else for that matter—the deeply personal choices about which such expression we, and our own young children, will see or not see. Unfortunately, when it comes to sexual expression, and only sexual expression, the Supreme Court has ignored all of the time-honored teachings of the *Cohen* case, and it has allowed government to punish one person's lyric just because it is another person's vulgarity.

III. Judge-created speech-suppressive doctrines to "justify" restrictions on sexual expression

In the area of sexual expression, the Supreme Court has unfortunately deviated from all of the general free-speech principles I have laid out, which have worked so well regarding speech with every other kind of content. The Court has allowed sexual expression to be singled out for regulation, and even outright banning, based only on its content. The Court has allowed sexual expression to be suppressed just because it is considered offensive by the majority of community members, elected officials, appointed FCC commissioners, or jury members.

The Court has not demanded any evidence that such expression causes any adverse impact at all, let alone a clear and present danger of great tangible harm that cannot be averted through any measures besides censorship. The great weight of the pertinent scholarship documents that there is no such evidence.[71] To the contrary, there is substantial evidence, which the Court has ignored, that the targeted sexual expression has many *positive* impacts, including for minors (at least older minors). Among other things, such expression provides valuable information about safer sex, contraception, and sexual orientation that promotes young people's health—and indeed can even be life-saving—given the rampant spread of HIV and other sexually transmitted diseases among teenagers, as well as the tragic spate of suicides among LGBT youth.[72]

The Court has created three major doctrines under which it permits suppression of sexual expression. One of these permits government to completely outlaw or criminalize some sexual expression, which the Court labels "obscenity." The other two doctrines permit government to strictly regulate other sexual expression in two contexts: the broadcast media[73] and adult entertainment establishments.[74] To distinguish this kind of restricted expression from the wholly banned category of obscenity, the Court usually calls such expression "indecency."

Obscenity

The very first time the Supreme Court considered whether sexual expression should be protected by the First Amendment's Free Speech Clause, the Court actually extolled the importance of such expression. In 1957, in a case called *Roth v. United States*,[75] the Court made what is probably its least controversial statement ever: "Sex, a great and mysterious motive force in human life, has indisputably been a subject of absorbing interest to mankind through the ages; it is . . . of . . . vital . . . human interest and public concern."[76] But no sooner had the Court said this than it proceeded to carve out from sexual expression a category that it held to be completely beyond the constitutional pale, labeling this pariah category "obscenity." This judge-made obscenity exception has been opposed by most constitutional scholars and by many Supreme Court Justices, including the very Justice who initially created it but who subsequently recanted that ruling. This exception was even opposed by a distinguished commission of academic experts that President Lyndon Johnson appointed way back in 1968.[77] Along with similar commissions in other countries,[78] these experts recommended constitutional protection for all sexual expression for all consenting adults.

In the 1973 case, *Paris Adult Theatre v. Slaton,* the whole Court acknowledged that "there are no scientific data which conclusively demonstrate that exposure to obscene material adversely affects men and women or their society."[79] Nonetheless, five Justices—a bare majority—asserted that such material could still be banned based on what they unabashedly called "unprovable assumptions" about its negative impacts on the moral "tone" of "a decent society."[80] Consistent with this rationale, the core of the Court-created obscenity concept states that local communities may ban material if they deem it to be "patently offensive."

Since that 1973 case, the Supreme Court has never again revisited the basic question of whether it should continue to enforce the obscenity exception to the First Amendment. However, in its free-speech juris-prudence since 1973, the Court has generally moved toward stronger and stronger enforcement of the fundamental content-neutrality principle, and it has even enforced that principle concerning sexual expression in many contexts other than the obscenity doctrine. Therefore, I believe that when the Court does finally revisit the obscenity exception, there is a strong chance that it will reject that exception altogether.

For many decades, the Supreme Court has tried but failed to come up with clear, objective standards for defining constitutionally unprotected obscenity. The most famous line in the Court's unsuccessful effort to define obscenity came from former Justice Potter Stewart when he candidly admitted, "I cannot define it, but I know it when I see it."[81] The problem, though, is that every judge, along with everyone else, sees a different "it"! Individuals even have different perspectives about whether any given expression has any sexual content at all. This is captured by the old joke about the man who sees every inkblot his psychiatrist shows him as wildly erotic. When his psychiatrist says to him, "You're obsessed with sex," the man answers: "What do you mean *I* am obsessed? *You* are the one who keeps showing me all these dirty pictures!"

Given our especially subjective views about the inherently personal realm of sex, this definitional problem persists no matter what sexual expression is targeted, under any rubric or any rationale. For example, as I have already noted, some feminists decry sexual expression that they view as demeaning or degrading to women. To distinguish this sexual expression from the long-established concepts of "obscenity" and "indecency," they label it with the stigmatizing term "pornography." In contrast, these anti-porn feminists use the term "erotica" for sexual expression that they do not deem degrading to women. How can you tell the difference, you might well ask? Well, as one feminist anti-pornography activist put it: "What turns *me* on is erotica; but what turns *you* on is pornography!"[82]

As the Supreme Court has recognized, freedom of speech is especially endangered whenever the government bans or regulates speech under broad, vague, subjective concepts such as "offensive."[83] Therefore, as I have repeatedly stressed, the Court has consistently invalidated censorship of non-sexual expression that targets "offensive" expression. Moreover, in the landmark 1997 case of *Reno v. ACLU*,[84] the Court struck down a federal law that censored sexual expression online, specifically because the law targeted "patently offensive" expression—a concept that the Court held to be overly broad and vague. This ruling is a key basis for my optimism that the Court will also repudiate both the obscenity doctrine and its old holdings allowing regulation of broadcast "indecency," because the definitions of both "obscenity" and broadcast "indecency" center on the "patently offensive" criterion.[85] Such vague concepts as "offensive" or "patently offensive" present a fundamental problem because they do not provide any clear, objective guidelines. These words allow police, prosecutors, and other enforcing officials to exercise their unfettered discretion according to their own subjective tastes or those of politically powerful community members. Consequently, the enforcement patterns will be arbitrary at best, discriminatory at worst. The situations that lead to particular expression being deemed offensive or obscene will be completely unpredictable.

This causes what courts call a "chilling effect"[86] because no one wants to run the risk of criminal prosecution. In other words, people self-censor and do not engage in expression just because it could be deemed offensive by the powers that be. That self-censorship not only violates the free-speech rights of all those who were deterred from speaking for fear of prosecution, but it also deprives the rest of us of the chance to hear valued expression, including constitutionally protected speech. The completely arbitrary, unpredictable nature of our current legal approach can best be illustrated by citing some recent examples of the FCC's enforcement of its broadcast indecency rules against particular words. I will simply list some of the contrasting rulings that the FCC issued in a single order. It held that "bullshit" *was* indecent, but that "dick" and "dickhead" were *not*. It held that non-explicit suggestions of teenagers' sexual activity in general *were* indecent, but that explicit discussions of specific teen sexual practices were *not*. It held that "fuck 'em" *was* indecent, but that "up yours" and "kiss my ass" were *not*.[87] As I noted above, the FCC also held that musicians' uses of "fuck" and "shit" in Martin Scorsese's documentary film about blues music *were* indecent. In contrast, it held that actors' uses of the very same words in the fictional film *Saving Private Ryan* were *not*.[88]

In response to these erratic rulings, no wonder we have seen so much self-censorship! The unfettered discretion involved in enforcing such vague concepts as "indecent," "offensive" or "obscene" is likely to be exercised in a manner that is not only arbitrary, but even worse, discriminatory, by singling out expression that is produced by or appeals to individuals or groups who are relatively unpopular or powerless. Indeed, recent obscenity prosecutions have targeted expressions of lesbian and gay sexuality[89] as well as rap music by young African-American men.[90]

Indecency

In addition to the obscenity concept, which allows the complete crimi-
nalization or banning of certain sexual expression, the Supreme Court
also has allowed strict regulation of other sexual expression—usually
called "indecency"—in two contexts. First, the Court has allowed such
expression to be barred from the broadcast airwaves during the time
when many minors are assumed to be in the audience, from 6 A.M. to
10 P.M.[91] Second, the Court has allowed businesses that purvey such
expression to be subjected to strict zoning laws. For example, adult
bookstores and strip clubs may be exiled to outlying areas of cities or
clustered together in a "red light district."[92] Along with the obscenity
exception, these indecency doctrines violate core free-speech principles and have been harshly criticized by many experts, including dis-
senting Justices.[93]

I am going to discuss in more detail only the first of these two indecency doctrines—indecency in broadcasting—since it is of more pervasive concern. Just as the Court's last decision that examined and upheld
the obscenity exception is more than 30 years old, the same is true of
the Court's last decision that examined and upheld the government's
power to restrict broadcast indecency. That decision, in *Pacifica v. FCC*,[94]
which I noted above, upheld the FCC's power to punish Pacifica Radio
for its daytime broadcast of George Carlin's famous "7 Dirty Words"
monologue. The *Pacifica* case was decided by a razor-thin 5–4 ruling,
and since then, it has been criticized by many other Justices.[95] Again,
this parallels the Court's 1973 ruling upholding the obscenity exception, which also was decided 5–4 and has since been criticized by many
other Justices. Moreover, *Pacifica* relied on factual premises about the
nature of broadcasting which—even if they were correct at the time—
are certainly no longer valid today. Specifically, the majority stressed
what it called the "uniquely pervasive nature of broadcast expression"
and its unique accessibility to young people.

Even if these factual conclusions were correct in 1971, they are certainly no longer true, given the subsequent explosion of so many other
media, which are at least as accessible to young people as broadcast television, and which the Court has held to be immune from special regulation, consistent with the First Amendment.[96] Yet, broadcasters can still
be severely fined, or even lose their broadcasting licenses, even though
the very same expression is completely insulated from regulation on the
very next channel if the next channel happens to be cable, rather than
broadcast. Surely it is past due time to end the second-class treatment

of the broadcast media along with the second-class treatment of sexual expression.

IV. Recent positive developments and ongoing law reform initiatives

That brings me to my fourth and final point: my positive prognosis about ending, or at least reducing, both kinds of disparity. As Woody Allen once told an audience: "I'd like to end with something positive, but I can't think of anything positive to say. Would you settle for two negatives?"[97]

I actually have many positives, but I will confine myself to the three that I consider the most important. First, in the recent past, the Supreme Court has strongly enforced the principle of content-neutrality even for the traditionally disfavored category of sexual expression. Therefore, I am cautiously optimistic that when the Court finally re-examines its current obscenity and indecency doctrines head-on, as it has not done for decades, it will reject these doctrines as completely inconsistent with the core content-neutrality principle. Second, the Court's landmark 2003 decision that strongly protects sexual *conduct, Lawrence v. Texas,*[98] also provides additional constitutional rationales for protecting sexual *expression* even beyond the free-speech content-neutrality principle. Third, the federal courts right now are re-examining the old cases that have rationalized suppression of broadcast "indecency," which is the first time they have done this in several decades, and the signs so far are encouraging.

Now I will expand a bit on that first positive development: the Court's recent strong enforcement of the core content-neutrality principle,[99] even concerning sexual expression. In a consistent line of cases, the Court has struck down restrictions on sexual expression in all new media, despite the government's arguments that these media should be relegated to the same second-class status as broadcast. The government has argued that the Court should use the same rationale that it used to uphold such broadcast restrictions back in the 1971 *Pacifica* case: namely, to shield children from "indecent" sexual expression they can easily access on these media. Although the Court has not yet directly overturned *Pacifica,* in every subsequent case it has read that precedent very narrowly and it has reached the opposite conclusion concerning every other medium it has considered. Accordingly, the Court has rejected restrictions on sexual expression on telephones (in the context of Dial-A-Porn);[100] on cable TV;[101] and on the Internet.[102] These decisions have been widely supported by Justices across the ideological spectrum and have been based on a robust concept of free speech that is completely at odds with the current obscenity and indecency doctrines.

The majority opinions in these recent cases have not expressly overruled any earlier cases, but I agree with the dissenters that the majority's rationales are inconsistent with prior precedents that did allow regulation of broadcast for the sake of shielding minors.[103] For example, in the most recent of these cases, involving cable TV, what the dissent stated as a reason to condemn the majority's ruling is to me a reason to praise it. Specifically, the dissent refers to what it sees as Congress's legitimate power to "help . . . parents . . . keep[ ] unwanted [sexual expression] from their children," and it then complains that "the Court reduces Congress's protective power to the vanishing point."[104] Hear, hear!

The second major positive development is the Supreme Court's historic 2003 decision in *Lawrence v. Texas*. Not only did the Court strike down the statute at issue—Texas's discriminatory ban on same-gender "sodomy" (oral or anal sex), but the Court also based its holding on broad-ranging rationales. Accordingly, this ruling should sound the death-knell for other laws that restrict other personal, private conduct by consenting adults, including their production or consumption of sexual expression. Most importantly, the Court reversed its infamous 1986 decision in *Bowers v. Hardwick*,[105] which had held that government may criminalize private, consensual adult conduct merely because the majority of the community disapproves of the conduct. That outdated concept reminds me of H.L. Mencken's famous definition of Puritanism: "the haunting fear that someone, somewhere, may be happy!"[106]

I cannot think of any supposed justification for criminal laws that is more antithetical to individual liberty. John Stuart Mill, in his classic 1859 essay, "On Liberty," said it best when he wrote, "Over himself, over his own body and mind, the individual is sovereign . . . [T]he only purpose for which government may rightfully exercise power . . . over anyone is to prevent harm to others. His own good, either physical or moral, is not a sufficient warrant."[107]

The Supreme Court's opinion in *Lawrence v. Texas* contains language that celebrates a similarly broad concept of individual freedom of choice, and I find this especially exciting, given that it was written by Justice Anthony Kennedy, a conservative, Republican Catholic, who was appointed by a conservative, Republican president, Ronald Reagan,[108] and who is the key swing vote on the current Court.[109]

One aspect of the *Lawrence* decision is of special significance in the ongoing effort to un-censor sexual expression. In overturning *Bowers,* the Court expressly held that laws cannot constitutionally be based only on majoritarian views about morality. This holding provoked a fierce tirade in Justice Scalia's strident dissent. He rightly recognized that this holding should doom a whole host of laws, far beyond the discriminatory anti-sodomy laws that were at issue in *Lawrence* itself. While this sweeping potential was the cause of Justice Scalia's consternation, for civil libertarians, it is cause for celebration! He wrote (emphasis mine):

> State laws [that are only based on moral choices include laws] against . . . nude dancing, same-sex marriage, prostitution, masturbation . . . fornication, and *obscenity* . . . Every single one of these laws is called into question by today's decision . . . This [decision] effectively decrees the end of all morals legislation.[110]

As I previously detailed, the 1973 Supreme Court decision upholding the obscenity exception reasoned that this exception was justified to preserve the "moral tone" of the community. Therefore, Justice Scalia was absolutely right in his *Lawrence* dissent when he said that the majority's rationale would warrant overturning the obscenity exception. In fact, one lower court ruling has held precisely that *Lawrence* does spell the death-knell for anti-obscenity laws. In that important ruling, federal judge Gary Lancaster, citing *Lawrence,* wrote, "Obscenity statutes [unconstitutionally] burden . . . individuals' fundamental right to possess, read, observe, and think about what [they] choose[] in the privacy of [their] own home."[111]

While an appellate court overturned that ruling,[112] it did not do so because it disagreed with Judge Lancaster's reading of *Lawrence.* Rather, the appellate court said that only the Supreme Court itself should directly apply its *Lawrence* holding to the obscenity context.[113] I am cautiously optimistic that, before long, the Supreme Court will do just that.

The third and final major positive development I will address is current litigation challenging the longstanding restrictions on broadcast "indecency." The silver lining to the cloud of the recent crackdowns on such expression is that they have spurred all the major broadcasters to unite in a frontal challenge to them. Moreover, many "friend of the court" briefs have been filed by many diverse opponents of the current repressive regime, including the one I mentioned earlier—none other than former FCC officials, one of whom had actually worked on the *Pacifica* case. That brief went so far as to call for a complete end to the regulation of broadcast indecency, as violating the First Amendment. The brief's ringing conclusion read:

> It is time to put an end to this experiment with indecency regulation . . . [I]t has [led to] a revival of Nineteenth Century Comstockery. As former regulators we appreciate that the FCC is in an uncomfortable position, buffeted by the turbulent passions of moral zealots and threats from over-excited Congressmen. But that is precisely why the matter must be taken out of the agency's hands entirely.[114]

In 2009, in *Fox v. FCC*,[115] the Supreme Court postponed addressing any of the fundamental constitutional questions about the increasingly anomalous second-class status that broadcast expression receives under the First Amendment. Instead, the Court narrowly ruled that the FCC did not violate administrative law principles when it recently reversed its own longstanding policy and began to sanction even "fleeting" or "isolated" expletives, including just a single four-letter word spontaneously uttered during a live performance. The Supreme Court reversed the Second Circuit's holding that the FCC had not adequately explained this policy change, and the high Court remanded the case for further proceedings.[116] Just as this chapter was going to press, on July 13, 2010, a three-judge panel of the U.S. Court of Appeals for the Second Circuit issued an opinion on remand that unanimously struck down the FCC's policy as violating the First Amendment. The court stressed a theme that this chapter also has highlighted: that the policy's vagueness creates a chilling effect that stifles much valuable expression.[117]

In the Supreme Court's 2009 *Fox* ruling, several of the Justices' opinions noted the unresolved First Amendment issues that would have to await future rulings by the Court. Indeed, as Justice Scalia's majority opinion observed, the Supreme Court would "perhaps" address these First Amendment issues at a later stage "in this very case."[118] In light of the Second Circuit's recent ruling, Justice Scalia's prediction seems likely to be fulfilled. Given the suppressive impact of the FCC's sweeping new concept of broadcast "indecency," it was disappointing that the Supreme Court in its 2009 *Fox* decision deferred ruling on the weighty First Amendment challenges to that concept. However, it was heartening that five Justices used their opinions to signal their sympathy to these challenges. Justice Thomas was the most critical, reiterating a point that he has made before, and calling into question the Court's prior rulings that permit more content regulation of broadcast than other media.[119] In addition, four other Justices indicated their receptivity toward First Amendment challenges: Justices Stevens,[120] Kennedy,[121] Ginsburg,[122] and Breyer.[123] Accordingly, I remain optimistic that the high Court will ultimately agree with the Second Circuit's recent forceful condemnation of the policy's sweeping censorial impact:

> [T]he absence of reliable guidance in the FCC's standards chills a vast amount of protected speech dealing with some of the most important and universal themes in art and literature. Sex and the magnetic power of sexual attraction are surely among the most predominant themes in the study of humanity since the Trojan War. The digestive system and excretion are also important areas of human attention. By prohibiting all "patently offensive" references to sex, sexual organs, and excretion without giving adequate guidance as to what "patently offensive" means, the FCC effectively chills speech, because broadcasters have no way of knowing what the FCC will find offensive. To place any discussion of these vast topics at the broadcaster's peril has the effect of promoting wide self-censorship of valuable material which should be completely protected under the First Amendment.[124]

In closing, I would like to share a passage from an opinion by former Supreme Court Justice William O. Douglas, who sat on the Court from 1939 to 1975 and who always dissented from all of the Court's cases denying full First Amendment protection to sexual expression.[125] This passage reflects Douglas's travels to Communist countries during the then-ongoing Cold War and it perfectly captures the First Amendment philosophy that should spell the end of sexual expression's second-class treatment. Justice Douglas wrote:

> 'Obscenity' . . . is the expression of offensive ideas. There are regimes in the world where ideas "offensive" to the majority . . . are suppressed. There life proceeds at a monotonous pace. Most of us would find that world offensive. One of the most offensive experiences in my life was a visit to a nation where bookstalls were filled only with books on mathematics and . . . religion. I am sure I would find offensive most of the [material] charged with being obscene. But in a life that has not been short, I have yet to be trapped into seeing or reading something that would offend me. . . . [O]ur society . . . presupposes that the individual, not government, [is] the keeper of his tastes, beliefs, and ideas. That is the philosophy of the First Amendment.[126]

Notes

1. This is a lightly edited version of oral remarks that Nadine Strossen delivered on March 3, 2007 (Keynote Address, University of Iowa, The 2007 Obermann Center for Advanced Studies, Humanities Symposium, "Obscenity: An Interdisciplinary Discussion"). It has been edited for the following purposes: (1) to convert it from oral speech format to essay format; (2) to add footnotes; and (3) to update it in terms of major pertinent developments between when the speech was delivered and when the published version was completed (July 2, 2010). Most of the work on these revisions was done by Professor Strossen's Senior Faculty Assistant Steven Cunningham (NYLS 1999) and her Research Assistant Trevor Timm (NYLS 2011).

2. See Katie Roiphe, "Date Rape's Other Victim," *New York Times,* June 13, 1993, at 40.

3. U.S. Constitution, amend. 1.

4. *Miller v. California,* 413 U.S. 15, 23–24 (1973).

5. *Collin v. Smith,* 578 F.2d 1197 (7th Cir. 1978).

6. *New York Times v. Sullivan,* 376 U.S. 254 (1964).

7. See *R. A. V. v. St. Paul,* 505 U.S. 377 (hate speech); *New York Times Co. v. Sullivan,* 376 U.S. 254 (1964) (defamatory falsehoods about government officials); and *Brandenburg v. Ohio,* 395 U.S. 444 (1969) (advocacy of violence and lawbreaking).

8. *Miller v. California,* 413 U.S. 15 (1973).

9. Alessandra Stanley, "A Flash of Flesh: CBS Again Is in Denial," *New York Times,* February 3, 2004 [originally used by Justin Timberlake to describe the incident].

10. Jack Shafer "The Case for killing the FCC and selling off spectrum," *Slate,* Jan. 17, 2007, http://www.slate.com/id/2157734.

11. Ibid.

12. Michelle Ingrassia, "We Must Improve Our Busts: We've Come a Long Way, Baby, on the Quest for Cleavage," *New York Daily News,* August 19, 2004.

13. Drew Clark, "A Bleeping Shame," *Congress Daily,* July 17, 2006.

14. *Fox TV Stations, Inc. v. FCC,* 489 F.3d 444, 458 (2d Cir. 2007).

15. Broadcast Indecency Enforcement Act, Public Law No. 235, 109th Congress, 2nd Sess. June 16, 2006.

16. Marisa Guthrie, "Indecency Law Threatens PBS. Fines Could Shut Down," *New York Daily News,* July 27, 2006.

17. Zay N. Smith, "Kiss, kiss, bang, bang and butt out," *Chicago Sun Times,* October 2, 2006.

18. Lawrence Van Gelder, "Arts, Briefly," *New York Times,* September 4, 2006.

19. "Vermont Public Radio Disinvites Candidate for Fear of Profanity," *Associated Press,* October 20, 2006.

20. "U.S. Senate Candidate Ejected, Arrested at Law School Debate," *Associated Press,* October 18, 2006.

21. U.S. Code vol. 47, sec. 231.

22. *American Civil Liberties Union v. Mukasey,* 534 F.3d 181, 207 (3d Cir. 2008).

23. *American Civil Liberties Union v. Gonzales,* 478 F. Supp.2d 775, 821 (E.D.Pa., 2007).

24. Federal Judicial Center, "Biographical Directory of Federal Judges: Lowel A. Reed," http://www.fjc.gov/servlet/tGetInfo?jid=1982 (The Honorable Lowell A. Reed, Jr., nominated by President Ronald Reagan on December 18, 1987, confirmed by Senate on April 19, 1988).

25. Federal Judicial Center, "Biographical Directory of Federal Judges: Morton Ira Greenberg, http://www.fjc.gov/servlet/nGetInfo?jid=912&cid=999&ctype=na&instate=na (The Honorable Morton Ira Greenberg, nominated by President Reagan on February 11, 1987, confirmed by Senate on March 23, 1987).

26. *Communications Decency Act* Passed House 414–16, Passed Senate 91–5; *Child Online Protection Act* Passed House 333–95 and Senate 65–29, Thomas.gov.

27. American Civil Liberties Union, "Freedom of Expression," http://www.aclu.org/freespeech/gen/21179pub20051031.html#6.

28. Dan Caterinicchia, "House OKs huge raise in indecency fine," *The Washington Times,* June 8, 2006.

29. Ibid.

30. The Free Expression Policy Project, "A Huge Victory For Free Speech on the Airwaves," June 4, 2007, http://www.fepproject.org/news/foxdecision.html.

31. *Communications Decency Act of 1996,* U.S. Code vol. 47, sec. 223(a)(1)(B)(ii); *Child Online Protection Act of 1998,* U.S. Code vol. 47, sec. 231(a)(1).

32. *Communications Decency Act* Passed House 414–16, Passed Senate 91–5, *Child Online Protection Act* Passed House 333–95 and Senate 65–29, Thomas.gov.

33. Al Kamen, "Gonzales' Curtain Call," *Washington Post,* January 5, 2005.

34. Dan Eggen, "Justice Department to Launch National Sex Offender Registry," *Washington Post,* May 20, 2005.

35. Larry Abramsom, "Federal Government Renews Effort to Curb Porn," *National Public Radio,* September 27, 2005, http://www.npr.org/templates/story/story.php?storyId=4865348.

36. Mark Follman, "The U.S. attorneys scandal gets dirty As Congress prepares to grill Alberto Gonzales, Salon has uncovered another partisan issue connected to the mass firings: Pornography," *Salon,* April 19, 2007, http://www.salon.com/news/feature/2007/04/19/DOJ_obscenity/.

37. Kay, Julie, "U.S. Attorney's Porn Fight Gets Bad Reviews Obscenity Prosecution Task Force will focus on Internet crimes and peer-to-peer distribution of pornography," *Daily Business Review.* August 30, 2005, accessed at http://www.law.com/jsp/article.jsp?id=1125318960389.

38. http://www.law.com/jsp/article.jsp?id=1125318960389.

39. Barton Gellman, "Recruits Sought for Porn-Squad," *Washington Post,* September 20, 2005.

40. Julie Kay, "U.S. Attorney's Porn Fight Gets Bad Reviews," *Daily Business Review,* August 30, 2005, http://www.law.com/jsp/article.jsp?id=1125318960389.

41. Mark Follman, "U.S. Attorneys Scandal Gets Dirty," *Salon,* April 19, 2007 http://www.salon.com/news/feature/2007/04/19/DOJ_obscenity.

42. See *American Civil Liberties Union v. Gonzales,* 478 F.Supp.2d 775 (E.D.Pa., 2007).

43. Tim Grieve and Farhad Manjoo, "Alberto Gonzales' hot pursuit of porn," *Salon,* February 16, 2005, http://www.salon.com/politics/war_room/2005/02/16/gonzales/index.html?source=search&aim=/politics/war_room.

44. Amanda Terkel, "Cuccinelli channels John Ashcroft, censors goddess' clothing on Virginia seal," *Thinkprogress.org,* May 1, 2010, http://thinkprogress.org/2010/05/01/cuccinelli-virginia-seal/.

45. U.S. Constitution, Amend. 1.

46. See, for example, Constitution of India, Part III, Section 19 (Protection of certain rights regarding freedom of speech); Canadian Charter of Rights and Freedoms, Part I (limitations clause); Irish Constitution Article 40.6.1.

47. Roy Jordan, "Free Speech and the Constitution," *Law and Bills Digest Group,* June 4,

2002, The Parliament of Australia, Parliamentary Library, Research Note Index 42 2001–02; Mark Rice-Oxley, "European Antiterror Laws Limit Free Speech," *The Christian Science Monitor,* Oct. 14, 2005.

48. Adam Liptak, "War of Words: For More Than 200 Years, Americans Have Revered the Constitution. So Why Can't We Agree On What It Means?," *New York Times,* September 5, 2005.

49. Ibid.

50. Tony Mauro, "High Court Deals First Amendment Wins, Losses: Analysis," FreedomForum.org, 2001–02, http://www.freedomforum.org/templates/document.asp?documentID=16535.

51. Nat Hentoff, *Freedom of Speech for ME, but not for THEE* (New York: HarperCollins, 1992).

52. *Madsen v. Women's Health Ctr.,* 512 U.S. 753 (U.S. 1994).

53. *Texas v. Johnson,* 491 U.S. 397 (1989).

54. *R.A.V. v. City of St. Paul, Minnesota,* 505 U.S. 377 (1992).

55. *United States v. Playboy Entm't Group,* 529 U.S. 803, 813 (2000).

56. *Brandenburg v. Ohio,* 395 U.S. 444 (1969).

57. *Whitney v. California,* 274 U.S. 357, 374–80 (1927).

58. *Schenk v. U.S.,* 249 U.S. 47 (1919).

59. *Gitlow v. N.Y.,* 268 U.S. 652, 673 (1925).

60. *Miller v. Civil City of South Bend,* 904 F.2d 1081 (1990).

61. Mary Kate McGowan, Conversational Exercitives and the Force of Pornography: A *Philosophy and Public Affairs* Reader, Princeton University Press, April 1, 2003.

62. E. R. Shipp, "Civil Rights Law Against Pornography Is Challenged," *New York Times,* May 15, 1984.

63. Stuart Taylor, Jr., "Pornography Foes Lose New Weapon in Supreme Court," *New York Times,* February 25, 1986.

64. See, for example, *American Booksellers Assoc. v. Hudnut,* 771 F.Supp. 1316 (1985); *American Booksellers Asso. v. Hudnut,* 771 F.2d 323, 329–30 (1985).

65. *American Booksellers Asso. v. Hudnut,* 771 F.2d 323, 329–30 (1985).

66. *Cohen v. California,* 403 U.S. 15 (1971).

67. *F.C.C. v. Pacifica,* 438 U.S. 726 (1978).

68. Federal Judicial Center, "Biographical Directory of Federal Judges: John Marshall Harlan," http://www.fjc.gov/servlet/nGetInfo?jid=979&cid=0&ctype=sc&instate=na (Nominated on November 8, 1954 by President Dwight Eisenhower, confirmed by Senate on March 16, 1955). http://www.supremecourthistory.org/02_history/subs_timeline/images_associates/075.html.

69. *Cohen v. California,* 403 U.S. 15, 24 (1971).

70. Ibid., 25.

71. Andrew Koppelman, "Free Speech and Pornography: A Response to James Weinstein," *New York University Review of Law & Social Change* 899 (2007); David Cole, "Playing by Pornography's Rules: The Regulation of Self Expression," *University of Pennsylvania Law Review* 143.111 (1994).

72. Planned Parenthood, "The Health Benefits of Sexual Expression," 2007, http://www.plannedparenthood.org/files/PPFA/fact-sexual-expression.pdf.

73. See, for example, *F.C.C. v. Pacifica,* 438 U.S. 726 (1978).

74. See, for example, *City of Renton v. Playtime Theatres,* 475 U.S. 41 (1986).

75. 354 U.S. 476, 487 (1957).

76. Ibid., 487.

77. "Obscenity Group Set Up," *Associated Press,* January 3, 1968.

78. Committee on Obscenity and Film Censorship, *Report of the Committee on Obscenity and Film Censorship: presented to Parliament by the Secretary of State for the Home Department by Command of Her Majesty* (London: November 1979).

79. *Paris Adult Theatre I v. Slaton,* 413 U.S. 49 (1973).

80. Ibid., 109.

81. *Jacobellis v. State of Ohio,* 378 U.S. 184, (1964).

82. Martin H. Levinson, "Review of: Defending Pornography: Free Speech, Sex, and the Fight for Women's Rights," *ETC.: A Review of General Semantics,* June 22, 1997. http://www. thefreelibrary.com/Defending+Pornography%3a+Free+Speech%2c+Sex%2c+and+the+ Fight+for+Women's . . . . -a020379935.

83. *Reno v. ACLU,* 521 U.S. 844 (1997).

84. Ibid.

85. *Ashwander v. Tennessee Valley Authority,* 297 U.S. 288 (1936).

86. See, for example, *Reno v. ACLU,* 521 U.S. 844, 872 (1997).

87. Federal Communications Commission, "In the Matter of Complaints Regarding Various Television Broadcasts Between February 2, 2002 and March 8, 2005," March 15, 2006, http://www.fcc.gov/eb/Orders/2006/FCC-06–17A1.html.

88. PBS, "FCC Crackdown on Indecency," *News Hour with Jim Lehrer* Transcript, March 16, 2006. http://www.pbs.org/newshour/bb/media/jan-june06/fcc_3–16.html.

89. Heidi Pike-Johnson, "First Principles—Adam Glasser Charged in Obscenity Case," *Reason,* Oct. 2001, http://findarticles.com/p/articles/mi_m1568/is_5_33/ai_78575520/.

90. Alana Samuels, "Sharpton to hit street to clean up rap," *L.A. Times,* May 3, 2007.

91. See, for example, *F.C.C. v. Pacifica,* 438 U.S. 726 (1978).

92. See, for example, *City of Renton v. Playtime Theatres,* 475 U.S. 41 (1986).

93. See, for example, *F.C.C. v. Pacifica,* 438 U.S. 726, 98 S.Ct. 3026 (1978); *F.C.C. v. Fox Television Stations, Inc.,* 129 S.Ct. 1800, 1820 (2009).

94. Ibid.

95. See, for example, *Federal Communications Commission v. Fox Television Stations, et al.,* 129 S.Ct. 1800 (2009).

96. See, for example, *Sable Communications of California, Inc. v. FCC,* 492 U.S. 115 (U.S. 1989); *United States v. Playboy Entm't Group,* 529 U.S. 803 (U.S. 2000); *Reno v. ACLU,* 521 U.S. 844 (1997).

97. Marc Engel, "Engaging the Wine Consumer," *Wine Business Monthly,* June 2007, http://www.winebusiness.com/html/MonthlyArticle.cfm?dataId=48586.

98. *Lawrence v. Texas,* 539 U.S. 558 (2003).

99. See *U.S. v. Stevens,* 130 S. Ct. 1577 (2010); *Citizens United v. Federal Election Commission,* 130 S. Ct. 876 (2010).

100. *Sable Communications of California, Inc. v. FCC,* 492 U.S. 115 (1989).

101. *United States v. Playboy Entm't Group,* 529 U.S. 803 (2000).

102. *Reno v. ACLU,* 521 U.S. 844, 117 S.Ct. 2329 (1997).

103. *United States v. Playboy Entm't Group,* 529 U.S. 803, 847 (2000).

104. Ibid.

105. *Bowers v. Harwick,* 478 U.S. 186 (1986).

106. *The Vintage Mencken,* ed. Alistair Cooke (New York: Vintage Books, 1956), chapter 47, p. 233.

107. J. S. Mill, *On Liberty* (London: John W. Parker & Son, West Strand [1859]), 9.

108. Federal Judicial Center, "Biographical Directory of Federal Judges: Anthony Kennedy," http://www.fjc.gov/servlet/nGetInfo?jid=1256&cid=0&ctype=sc&instate=na (President Reagan nominated him as an Associate Justice of the Supreme Court, and he took his seat February 18, 1988). http://www.supremecourtus.gov/about/biographiescurrent. pdf.

109. Tony Mauro, "Third Parties Shielded from Securities Suits," *New York Law Journal,* January 16, 2008.

110. *Lawrence v. Texas,* 539 U.S. 558, 599 (2003).

111. *United States v. Extreme Assocs.,* 352 F. Supp. 2d 578, 595–96 (W.D. Pa. 2005), *rev'd,* 431 F.3d 150 (3d Cir. 2005).

112. *U.S. v. Extreme Associates, Inc.,* 431 F.3d 150 (3d Cir. 2005).

113. Ibid., 161.

114. Brief for Former FCC Officials as Amici Curiae Supporting Petitioners, Fox Television Stations, Inc., 2006 WL 5100104, 24–26 (2d Cir. 2006).

115. *F.C.C. v. Fox Television Stations, Inc.,* 129 S.Ct. 1800 (2009).

116. *F.C.C. v. Fox Television Stations, Inc.,* 489 F.3d 444 (2d. Cir. 2007).

117. *Fox Television Stations, Inc. v. F.C.C.,* 2010 U.S. App. LEXIS 14293 (2ᵈ Cir. 2010).

118. *F.C.C. v. Fox Television Stations, Inc.,* 129 S.Ct. 1800, 1819 (2009).

119. Ibid., 1820 ("Red Lion and Pacifica [two Supreme Court decisions according lesser First Amendment protection to broadcast expression] were unconvincing when they were issued, and the passage of time has only increased doubt regarding their continued validity . . . Red Lion adopted, and Pacifica reaffirmed, a legal rule that lacks any textual basis in the Constitution).

120. Ibid., 1828 ("While Justice Thomas and I disagree about the continued wisdom of Pacifica, the changes in technology and the availability of broadcast spectrum he identifies certainly counsel a restrained approach to indecency regulation, not the wildly expansive path the FCC has chosen").

121. Ibid., 1826 ("I agree with the Court that as this case comes to us from the Court of Appeals we must reserve judgment on the question whether the agency's action is consistent with the guarantees of the Constitution").

122. Ibid., 1829 ("If the reserved constitutional question reaches this Court, see ante, at 1819 (majority opinion), we should be mindful that words unpalatable to some may be 'commonplace' for others, 'the stuff of everyday conversations'").

123. Ibid., 1832 (". . . two Members of the majority [in Pacifica] suggested that they could reach a different result, finding an FCC prohibition unconstitutional, were that prohibition aimed at the fleeting or single use of an expletive").

124. 2010 U.S. App. LEXIS 14293, *51–52.

125. *Ginzburg v. U.S.,* 86 S.Ct. 969 (1966).

126. *Paris Adult Theatre I v. Slaton,* 413 U.S. 49, 71 (1973).

"Guessing Oneself into Jail"

Morris Ernst and the Assault on
American Obscenity Laws in the 1930s

Morris Leopold Ernst's name elicits little recognition today, except from those who know the histories of American literary censorship, the birth control movement in the Margaret Sanger era, the early decades of the ACLU, and, to a lesser extent, the history of liberal anticommunism in the United States. Yet a leading scholar in the field of book history declared Ernst the most important unstudied figure in twentieth-century American cultural history.[1] So who is this forgotten but vital figure?

Ernst was arguably the nation's most prominent civil liberties lawyer in the late 1920s and 30s, known especially for his challenges to obscenity law at the local, state, and federal levels. By the eve of World War II, no one in the United States had done more to thwart censors' attacks on a variety of cultural forms, from literature to nudism, burlesque theatre, and radio—and no one had done more to rationalize birth-control laws, either. A prolific, self-promoting author of middlebrow works about the excesses of "Comstockery" in all its forms, Ernst wrote or co-wrote twenty-one books, a handful championing the emerging liberal anti-censorship tradition he did much to develop and articulate.[2]

Ernst gained his greatest fame for his defense of literary modernist texts, including Radclyffe Hall's *Well of Loneliness* (1929) and, most famously, James Joyce's *Ulysses* (1933), and was a towering figure in the history of American battles over obscenity law and censorship until the

Cold War.[3] He began earning his reputation as the nation's foremost obscenity law expert when he co-authored an influential history of obscenity law titled *To the Pure* (1928), and in the next half-dozen years he compiled a truly impressive series of legal victories in federal, state, and New York city courts on obscenity matters.[4]

Although he was not the first civil libertarian to take on local and federal obscenity laws and their agents, he was the most systematic and successful by far until a new generation of lawyers took on these issues in the late 1950s.[5] Neutralizing the legal arguments and cultural rationale behind the enforcement of Victorian-era obscenity laws, and ridiculing the symbolically potent censors who enforced cultural and legal "Comstockery," Ernst deserves recognition as the legal midwife to literary and sexual modernism in the U.S. for his work against obscenity laws.[6]

As a central part of his strategic assault on obscenity laws, Ernst also orchestrated important test cases to advance knowledge of human sexuality and to give women greater control over their reproductive lives. Between 1929 and 1937, he and his associates in the New York law firm Greenbaum, Wolff, and Ernst won five federal court cases challenging Customs Bureau and Post Office censorship practices over sex hygiene and education materials and birth-control information barred under the authority of the 1873 Comstock laws. Defending the importation of books authored by British birth-control activist Marie Stopes in two Customs Bureau cases, the mailing of American sexologist Mary Ware Dennett's sex hygiene pamphlet, and the receipt of birth-control devices and information by the Birth Control Federation of America (BCFA) associates of Margaret Sanger, Ernst devoted his strategic vision and legal expertise to reproductive rights law. He maintained a long relationship with Sanger as her counsel and as general counsel to the BCFA, later named Planned Parenthood.[7]

By the eve of World War II, when his energy and political focus shifted to war-related matters and the cause of anti-communism, Ernst had, for over a decade, battled the cultural practices, legal logic, and administrative apparatus of the anti-obscenity forces in New York City, New York State, and the federal government. In the courts, and in the court of public opinion, Ernst and his associates, especially Harriet Pilpel and Alexander Lindey, dismantled the assumptions undergirding obscenity laws in the United States as they had evolved in the late nineteenth and early twentieth centuries, persuading the courts that the nineteenth-century obscenity laws and standards were outdated to meet the needs of a diverse, modern public and were altogether too vague to meet the standards of legal precision necessary to modern jurisprudence. Although this essay will detail a host of arguments that Ernst and his associates wielded to diminish the strength and breadth of obscenity laws, I'll suggest here that seven main arguments were central to his successful assault:

- First, sexual morality had evolved considerably from the mid-nineteenth century, when the Comstock laws were conceived, to the 1930s, and the legal standards for obscenity needed to evolve to reflect an increasingly diverse, urbane society and citizenry with competing and not uniform interests or moral codes.

- Second, the courts needed to reconsider who the general reader was and what that reader needed to be protected from; that rather than defending the typically female and vulnerable reader, or the pathological or imbecilic reader, the courts needed to think of the general reader as a rational, mature, adult stable in his or her beliefs and behavior.

- Third, the Courts needed to recognize the necessity of drawing upon literary experts on questions of literary quality and matters of experimentation in the field of literature in general, and not leave these matters up to the tastes or common sense of judges and juries untrained to assess modern literature.

- Fourth, books should be read as a whole, rather than as mere parts, and that doing so would show that individual incidents of sexual morality or immorality were incidental to larger developments of character, fate, and plot, rather than merely titillating parts.

- Fifth, the courts needed to have demonstrated some actual evidence of danger and harm, rather than accept the state's claims of audience vulnerability to harm because of potential encounters with "obscene" materials.[8]

- Sixth, by accepting as "scientific" and necessary to a modern public the reputable sexology literature dealing with masturbation and married sexual pleasure, and protecting the right of certain classes of recipients—namely, married women and their licensed physicians—to have access to birth-control information and technologies, the courts would satisfy core needs of the modern public, especially the modern family.

- And seventh, even though the First Amendment does not protect obscenity per se, the still operative nineteenth-century obscenity statutes were in derogation of the Bill of Rights, in spirit.

Together with these central arguments, Ernst and others bundled together a cluster of additional arguments that over time produced a persuasive legal and cultural counter-attack to the increasingly defensive censorship agents, both local and national.[9]

His obvious promotional and legal talents made him a valuable, much-utilized resource for progressive political and cultural causes, and his law firm became a vital resource as well. Through earlier association with the ACLU's founder, Roger Baldwin, Ernst became an officer on the Executive Board of the ACLU, serving from 1927–54. He became General Counsel to the Union's national office by 1929 and held that position through the tumult of the 1930s, 40s, and early 50s. As executive board member and counsel, Ernst helped deploy the ACLU's resources for anti-censorship causes and was instrumental in bringing sexuality and obscenity matters into the ACLU's sphere of concerns. The Union actively promoted and publicized Ernst's efforts and occasionally helped subvent his firm's legal costs.[10]

Ernst had a wide range of legal and political interests beyond the literary and the sexual, and he developed a consistent set of principles about the right to speak and the importance of the public's access to a rich and diverse "marketplace of thought." He engaged in a range of causes promoting freedom of expression, including becoming counsel to the American Newspaper Guild, defending the right of journalists for collective bargaining; being counsel to actors in the Dramatists Guild and counsel to the burlesque theatre industry, where he fought many battles with the Commissioner of Licenses in New York City over closings of both "legitimate" and burlesque theaters; co-founding the National Lawyers Guild; and being appointed a member of President Truman's Committee on Civil Rights. And throughout his career he was one of the most insistent critics of oligopoly conditions in the mass communications industries, paying special attention to consolidation of the radio and film industries, the decimation of locally owned newspapers by the newspaper chains, and postal rates that hindered market access to small newspaper and magazines and created bottlenecks in the flow of creativity and ideas necessary to a healthy democracy.[11]

In all, Ernst came to understand obscenity-law restrictions in light of a larger political, cultural, and intellectual commitment to a well-informed, rational public, the necessity of a vigorous marketplace of ideas, and a legal system not cluttered by vague moralistic language and unproven assertions of harm to an undifferentiated, susceptible public.

At battle with obscenity laws

The first federal obscenity law in the United States, passed in 1842, authorized the Customs Service to confiscate "obscene or immoral" pictures, and by the time of the American Civil War (1861–65), widespread obscenity statutes were on the books in the individual states. Most of these statutes shared an English Common Law language and set of assumptions, especially that common law prohibited "whatever outrages decency and is injurious to public morals." In 1868, in the British case of *Regina v. Hicklin,* Lord Chief Justice Cockburn articulated a definition of obscenity that shaped obscenity law in English and American courts—in the U.S. until the 1930s.[12] The *Hicklin* standard, which American courts almost immediately adopted from the British, turned on whether "the tendency of the matter charged as obscenity is to deprave and corrupt those whose minds are open to such immoral influences, and into whose hands a publication of this sort *may* fall." This broad, conditional language was a prosecutor's dream: It required proof only that a work could be interpreted as obscene and required neither demonstration of ill intent nor actual harm to readers or viewers. This loose standard of causality accepted strong moralistic assertions of probable or possible effects as sufficient evidence of potentially damaging effects, especially to the young and vulnerable.[13]

In the United States, the cultural and legal assault on obscene materials accelerated dramatically after 1873, when the now infamous Anthony Comstock, Secretary of the New York Society for the Suppression of Vice and the leading advocate of efforts to stamp out offensive materials, persuaded Congress to expand the federal obscenity law. The 1873 federal "Comstock Law" barred sending through the mails not only "any obscene, lewd, or lascivious book, pamphlet, picture, print, or other publication of vulgar and indecent character," but also "any article or thing designed or intended for the prevention of conception or procuring of abortion." By specifically adding birth-control information and devices to the list of banned materials, the law effectively extended federal jurisdiction into all matters relating to reproduction and put the authority of Postal and Customs officials behind efforts to surveil the mails.[14]

The Supreme Court upheld the constitutionality of the Comstock Act in a series of late-nineteenth-century cases, and local and federal courts routinely employed the language of the Hicklin standard of "proof." Books and other materials were prosecuted or banned not for their actual effects, but rather for their *possible effects* on anyone who might conceivably read or encounter them—especially children, young men and women (particularly the latter), or the mentally weak. This meant, for instance, that even medical materials about contraception or abortion, aimed at doctors and medical students, could be, and were, found obscene because they might fall into the hands of the susceptible classes. As long as the prosecutors could prove the "obscenity" of an artifact, there were no First Amendment concerns, because the First Amendment gave no protection to obscene materials.[15]

In short, from the Civil War era until the 1930s, accurate scientific information about married sex, adolescent sexuality, masturbation, homosexuality, reproduction, abortion, and birth control was consistently deemed obscene and kept out of the mails and bookstores to prevent it from falling into the hands of susceptible audiences.[16]

At battle with the Vice Society

Ernst's autobiographic statements indicate that his interests in obscenity matters began to crystallize in 1927 after losing a U.S. Customs obscenity case in defense of a small bookseller arrested by agents of the New York Society for the Prevention of Vice for selling an obscene book, John Hermann's *What Happens.*[17] Ernst subsequently became obsessed with fighting local and federal obscenity laws, and with doing battle against John M. Sumner, the New York Vice Society heir to the notorious Anthony Comstock. Sumner stood for a particularly repressive Victorianism, and his underhanded tactics against booksellers and publishing houses galled and motivated Ernst. Ernst proved a quick study, co-writing an influential history of obscenity law in 1928 titled *To the Pure,* a thoroughgoing attack on Comstockery as an intellectual and cultural offense, and a useful legal primer for others interested in such battles.[18] Through his successes defending local booksellers in the New York City Magistrates Courts, and his strategic victories in the federal courts, by the early 1930s he quickly achieved national recognition as the most effective anti-censorship strategist.

Ernst, Pilpel, Lindey, and others in the Greenbaum, Wolff, and Ernst firm, developed a broad anti-censorship agenda and undertook a decade-long assault on obscenity laws. That agenda became increasingly strategic and focused on orchestrating winnable test cases on matters dealing with human sexuality, literary and cultural modernism, and the right of access to birth-control information and technology. They won by convincing judges and juries that the vague overreaching language of the obscenity laws and the cultural arguments leveled against sexual, literary, and artistic modernism were outmoded and anathema to evolving standards of legal evidence and to the needs of a diverse, urbane public. Although he was not the first American lawyer to make these arguments, Ernst had the greatest success making them in local and federal courts.[19]

Given his growing interest in obscenity law, Ernst functioned as counsel to leading publishing houses (including Random House and Putnam) and to more adventurous smaller firms committed to publishing provocative works (including Vanguard and Viking). He became defense counsel to many of New York City's booksellers routinely hassled by John M. Sumner and his smut hounds,[20] and from the late 1920s through the mid-1930s he and his anti-censorship allies were in constant local skirmishes with Sumner's Vice Society, winning decision after decision in the local Magistrates Courts in defense of booksellers for selling, among other works, Arthur Schnitzler's *Casanova's Homecoming*, George Moore's *A Storyteller's Holiday*, and Gustave Flaubert's *November*, to name just a few.[21] Ernst and his allies in the growing anti-censorship movement—including the ACLU's affiliate organization, the National Commission on Freedom From Censorship—actively publicized each and every battle with and victory over Sumner. Along the way, they actively sought out battles to publicize their cause and Sumner's tactics.

They had the perfect foil in John M. Sumner, who led the Vice Society crusades against what he perceived as the cultural degradation wrought by sexual license and modern culture. Sumner tried to hold the line against the obscene in the world of literature and art, and in so doing he frequently resorted to underhanded means to achieve arrests and seize stockpiles of booksellers' books; these tactics infuriated Ernst, especially because even after booksellers were exonerated in the courts, Sumner frequently failed to return, or considerably delayed returning, the seized stockpiles. The result deepened the antipathy between Ernst and Sumner, and the growing animus is an important part of the atmosphere and official record of this period of censorship history. Ernst made Sumner his whipping boy in the press and routinely ridiculed him both publicly and in his trial briefs. He and his anti-censorship allies orchestrated specific censorship events to create book-seizure spectacles that were sure to dramatize Sumner's methods and his anti-modernism, facilitating Ernst's purposes of bringing down censorship barriers and promoting the anti-censorship cause in the name of intellectual freedom and the marketplace of thought.

Ernst was strategic in cultivating his battles with federal authorities as well, and his lasting claim to fame—his victory over Customs officials in the 1933 *Ulysses* case—was a long planned and hoped-for outcome of a series of cases he set in motion with the 1929 *Well of Loneliness* case. His anti-censorship ally, Lewis Gannett, book critic and columnist for the *New York Herald,* chronicled Ernst's local and federal victories from 1927–33, locating the *Ulysses* decision within Ernst's larger assault on obscenity law. While touting Ernst's body of work and celebrating the prize of the *Ulysses* case, Gannett also illustrates the strategic, promotional relationship Ernst developed with book critics and journalists who were lined up with him on the anti-censorship, anti-Sumner front. Celebrating the victories over Sumner, without ever mentioning Sumner directly, Gannett writes:

> The tide really turned about the time that Morris Ernst, attorney, who has fought most of the historic censorship cases of the last five years . . . lost a censorship case the previous year (1927). . . . The defeat aroused a crusading zeal in Mr. Ernst. He dug into the history of censorship, published his books exposing its absurdities and contradictions, and emerged as the logical and fearless defender of frank, honest literature.
>
> In 1929, with Mr. Ernst as defending counsel in both cases, Radclyffe Hall's *The Well of Loneliness* was cleared of the charge of obscenity in General Sessions, and Magistrate Gottlieb gave [Schnitzler's] *Casanova's Homecoming* a clean-cut endorsement. In 1930 the Circuit Court of Appeals reversed an adverse verdict of a lower court on Mary Ware Dennett's *The Sex Side of Life,* and Judge Woolsey, in the first of three decisions which have become historic, ruled in favor of Dr. Marie Stopes's *Married Love.* . . . An amazing series of amazing victories for Morris Ernst.
>
> The *Ulysses* decision is the culmination of a long struggle for sanity. Judge Woolsey's decision is not necessarily binding on the state courts of this and still less of other states, nor are the little censors of the Post Office Department officially bound by it. But the large scope, the careful wording and thinking of Judge Woolsey's previous decisions have had their effect on other courts, and the *Ulysses* decision is sure to prove a monument.[22]

As Gannett indicated, Ernst's work on literary materials was not separable from his defense of materials about human sexuality or from his commitment to rationalizing federal law concerning both cultural expression and reproductive matters.

While Sumner was not the only censor with whom Ernst cultivated tactical skirmishes, their ongoing battles perfectly embody the clash of the modern with the passing mores of late Victorian culture. Ernst was astutely aware of the importance of public opinion, and by choosing cases that could be used to good public-relations advantage (Sumner's seizure of books by Schnitzler, Moore, and Flaubert are cases in point), he cultivated and drew upon an audience and supporting chorus of literary reviewers and noted authors and was able to routinely use Sumner to excellent effect as his foil. But the antagonism was real, and Ernst developed a kind of missionary zeal in defeating Sumner and in changing the censorship laws and practices of New York City and the nation.

Although by the early 1930s he was consistently losing his obscenity prosecutions in the New York City Magistrates Courts, Sumner nonetheless argued that he exerted considerable marketplace force by threatening booksellers with prosecutions and thereby driving them to stop the sale of books, even forcing some out of business. Sumner contended that he was more successful than Ernst and others gave him credit for, and that they exaggerated his failures and his excesses in their publicity campaigns against him. But Ernst invoked marketplace arguments as well, combining his marketplace of thought argument with claims of literary reputation and the sexual information needs, or interests, of the modern adult audience. He also evaded the cultural degradation argument voiced by Sumner by not defending (for the most part) the truly smutty and disreputable materials, choosing instead to fight on behalf of reputable, defensible works, to achieve a winning record whose cumulative force was itself an argument about changing legal and public tastes.

Ernst's marketplace arguments pointed both to consumers' interest and public taste, on the consumption end, and to production, represented by the entire book industry, including publishers, booksellers, and book reviewers. For Ernst the sales and distribution of works were evidence that the commercial marketplace reflected the evolution of public interests, tastes, and needs; and the fact that a disputed book was advertised, reviewed in important newspapers, stocked and circulated in leading bookstores everywhere meant that it had been accepted, even approved, by the contemporary community. Sumner countered that this appeal to the publishing industry and its marketplace was morally evasive and obtuse, and that commercial culture and public taste should not be the arbiters of where public morals should be. Sumner expressly linked literary people with abnormality and argued that the judgments of abnormal people should not determine and guide the public's moral standards.

Sumner attacked the frankness of modern literature, especially its so-called realism, by arguing that it was leading the reading public toward a fetid sewer of taste and dissipation. When defending more problematic works—sexually frank and marked by social realism—Ernst explained them to judges and juries as cautionary tales. Literary works replete with sordid details and sexual frankness could be, he argued, instructive morality tales, and not just tawdry fare. Nothing in the sordid environments and the generally downward trajectories of the central characters' lives should be construed as being attractive to the average reader, he argued. The fact that the protagonists' lifestyles were unattractive was not a hindrance to their defense; rather, they were realistic depictions of modern life as lived by some people. Additionally, Ernst successfully argued that those particular passages depicting sexual desire and fulfillment should be read as part of a larger whole, with sexual frankness as utterly true to life, and the specific episodes as incidental to the larger narrative. The Magistrates Court judges were quite persuaded by this interpretive framework and frequently reproduced this logic in their decisions.

The Ernst–Sumner clashes were carried out in the city's newspapers and its courts, and Ernst usually won. He did so by directly challenging the moralistic, but not necessarily demonstrable, assertions used in obscenity prosecutions about youth and their vulnerabilities, about unleashing public pathologies, and about rotting moral foundations. To counter these, Ernst argued about the need for frank, instructive materials, about the rational capacities of the reading public, and about the potentially salubrious effects of sociological realism for a modern audience. But most crucially, he argued about the unacceptable vagueness of obscenity law and its standards of evidence. Ernst took these arguments into other arenas of obscenity law, where he also met with considerable success.

In all of these cases—literary, sex hygiene and education, and birth control—Ernst's core legal arguments and publicity campaigns recurred to a series of questions about harm: How harmful are the supposedly obscene materials? Whom they will harm? How can that harm be assessed? Do nineteenth-century moral assumptions about harm meet twentieth-century definitions of morality? Do the so-called obscene materials meet public interests and needs? And, if so, what materials should the adult majority be denied because a potentially vulnerable minority might be harmed? His adroitness at forcing legal authorities to answer these questions with the precision required of modern jurisprudence produced a series of legal victories, creating important openings for cultural and sexual modernism.

So, too, he addressed the problem of audience vulnerability, which was inseparable from the question of harm. Because harm and vulnerability were both legal criteria and moral claims, they were at the very center of the obscenity discourse. For Ernst and others fighting obscenity laws, the core question was this: Who gets constructed as the vulnerable audience/consumer? The young, generally female, and sexually vulnerable? The young, impressionistic, and potentially predatory male? Or the average adult? Under Ernst's and others' persuasion, the New York City Magistrates Court judges, and eventually the federal court judges, came to understand that the average adult reader was the operative consumer in the literary and sexual modernist marketplace. This shift in the vulnerable-audience argument became a critical turning point in the successful legal defense of "obscene" literature, birth control, and sex hygiene materials, as the moral claim of potential harm became less persuasive when adult men—and not youth in general, especially teenaged girls—were constructed as the presumed audience. The assumption that the average audience was not vulnerable, and was capable of refraining from the kinds of behaviors depicted in even the most questionable texts was central to undermining obscenity prosecutions. Once stable adults replaced vulnerable youth as the assumed audience, prosecutors found it very difficult to win obscenity prosecutions unless the works on trial were well beyond the pale of contemporary sensibility.

Ernst's trial and appellate briefs, where most of these arguments were articulated in case after case, weren't just legal arguments; rather, they were essays that spoke to the social and cultural ruptures of the moment. His briefs, and his published works, were persuasive essays about contemporary laws fitting the needs of a modernizing public, under the guarantees of a legal system that could and should offer more protection for freedom of inquiry, for the dissemination of useful information, and for greater semantic and administrative precision on the part of the state if it was going to interfere with the flow of ideas.

Ernst was particularly forceful about the imprecise language of the obscenity statutes, given shifting cultural tastes and mores. He highlighted how statutory vagueness became a weapon wielded by prosecutors, and made the imprecision of obscenity laws indefensibly evident. The problem with obscenity laws, especially the "deprave and corrupt" language, was that they were based on prosecutors', juries', and judges' subjectivity, subjectivities that were rooted in variables such as educa-

tional background, religion, or attitudes about sex. These were profoundly imprecise terms. Ernst essentially argued that in strict legal
terms, there must be a standard of conduct that is possible to know
and to be tested against. As he wrote to a colleague in preparation for
trial, "Obscenity still remains the only crime the determination of which
depends essentially on speculation, not on facts or known standards."
But because of the utter vagueness of the obscenity statutes, knowing
the line that distinguished the obscene from the not obscene was nearly
impossible and utterly necessary in a just legal system. "It is obvious that
any element of vagueness and uncertainty is hostile to the fundamental principles of justice and places an individual at the mercy of mere
chance. If definiteness is essential to law in general, it is doubly so to
criminal law; it should be made impossible for a man to guess himself
into jail."[23]

Sexual modernism

Ernst should be just as well remembered for his defenses of sex-information materials and birth control as for his defenses of literature.
Between the Radclyffe Hall Customs Bureau case over *The Well of Loneliness* in 1929 and the *Ulysses* decision in 1933, Ernst won three federal
court trials on questions of disseminating "obscene" materials about
human sexuality through Customs and the Postal system. Then in the
mid-1930s he won two more federal trials on Customs and Postal control over birth-control materials.

As he gained focus on the defense of literary and cultural expression, he also turned to the defense of information about human sexuality. In the most famous and highly publicized of his sex-information
cases (due in part to the ACLU's fundraising and promotional work),
Ernst eventually regained for Mary Ware Dennett the right to use the
mails to distribute her widely used, well-respected pamphlet "The
Sex Side of Life." The trial over Dennett's pamphlet, which was used
primarily for the sexual education of youth, put modern youth and
access to information about sexuality on trial. Because she dared to
write frankly about masturbation as normal, and not morally fraught,
and about sex as pleasurable and sexual feelings as natural, she was
accused, and initially found guilty, of trafficking in obscene materials.
The core cultural anxieties about youth, masturbation, and the breakdown of self-discipline and chastity as the bulwark of moral order suffused the discussions surrounding the case, and Dennett's repudiation

of the literature and folklore against masturbation (with its warnings of madness, infirmity, and licentiousness leading to self-destruction) was the central issue for both those defending and those opposing her. Ernst, the ACLU, and others actively publicized the case, and in March 1930 Ernst succeeded in convincing the federal appellate court to overturn a lower federal court conviction for distributing obscene materials through the mail.[24]

Fresh from this victory, he approached British birth-control activist (and eugenicist) Marie Stopes about taking on the Customs Bureau ban on the importation of two of her books, one her advice manual *Married Love,* and the other her birth-control book, titled *Contraception.*[25] Like the Dennett case, the Stopes trials marked important legal challenges to an older moral order, and the growing legal recognition of the right of the modern adult public to have access to frank, scientific information about sexuality and its pleasures, and reproduction and its control, especially for married couples. Ernst won these two federal court cases against the Customs Bureau in 1931.

Not coincidentally, at the time Ernst was defending Mary Ware Dennett, he also began working as counsel for Margaret Sanger (Dennett's erstwhile leadership rival in the inchoate American birth-control movement), defending the 16th Street Birth Control Clinic against a raid and seizure of all records by the New York City police. Thus began Ernst's and his law firm's long association with Sanger and birth-control activists, including Ernst's efforts at mediating relations between Sanger and Dennett, who had very different ideas about the goals, strategies, and leadership of the birth-control movement. For the progressive sexual modernists such as Dennett, Sanger, and Stopes, and for Ernst and his colleagues, especially Harriet Pilpel—a longtime counsel for the birth-control movement—the issues of sexual pleasure and knowledge could not be separated from the issue of the right of reproductive control.[26]

He and his colleagues targeted the broad authority that the Comstock Act's "obscenity" language gave to Customs officials, Postal officers, and local prosecutors to interfere with the adult public's right of access to information about sexuality and reproduction. Ernst, Pilpel, and Lindey made their firm the most important law firm in the country on birth-control matters in the 1930s and 40s, when the birth-control movement was dramatically expanding. Following their defense of Sanger's clinic against police raids in 1929, they won two mid-1930s federal birth-control cases about the right of licensed physicians and scientific researchers to have access to birth-control technology (*United States v. One Package of Japanese Pessaries,* 1936), and contraceptive information

(*U.S. v. Norman E. Himes,* 1937).[27] As with the literature cases, Ernst and his firm orchestrated these as test cases, hoping to ensure that the federal government could not deny birth-control information and devices to licensed physicians, clinics, druggists, and scientific researchers interested in these matters.

In all, Ernst and associates won five federal cases between 1931 and 1937 (including the two Stopes cases and Dennett), dramatically diminishing the broad reach of obscenity restrictions on reputable, modern, scientific information about human sexuality and reproduction. For birth-control advocates this meant that doctors could prescribe contraceptives to preserve the lives and protect the health of their married patients (unless proscribed by state laws), and that federal postal and customs officials could not interfere with distribution or dissemination of materials addressed to the "privileged class" of recipients—namely, licensed professionals.[28] For the birth-control movement, there was plenty more work to be done, but Ernst's legal work in the 1930s went a long way toward rationalizing and regularizing federal law on birth-control matters. By the eve of World War II, no one in the United States had done more than Morris Ernst to expand legal protection to a variety of cultural forms, from literature and art to nudism, theatre, film, and radio—and no one had done more to rationalize birth-control laws, either.

Conclusion

To conclude, I want to do two things. First, I want to provide a summation of the cumulative defense strategy Ernst developed in his prime years defending literary and sexual modernism in the New York and federal courts. Second, I want to put some clay on Ernst's feet, lest this essay have the effect of leaving this problematic figure with the glow of unabashed hagiography.

Ernst's many trial briefs during this period made a series of legal and cultural arguments that were repeated and elaborated in subsequent cases as his defenses grew more numerous. Individually and collectively, the briefs embraced a narrative trajectory about cultural progress and sexual liberation from the nineteenth century to the late 1920s–30s and the growing tolerance of an increasingly cosmopolitan and sophisticated judiciary whose understanding of the modern condition outpaced the Victorian sensibilities of the censors. In short, Ernst argued the following:

- Sexual morality had evolved considerably from the mid-nineteenth century.
- John Sumner's obsessions were pathological, old-fashioned, and disturbed, and his tactics were underhanded, relying on such subterfuge as the use of undercover agents.
- The Vice Society's failure to achieve any pattern of success in prosecuting books in the late 1920s and 30s was due in part to the New York City Magistrates Courts' cosmopolitan rationality and willingness to entertain more complex and evolving understandings of morality and taste.
- The legal standards for obscenity need to evolve to reflect an increasingly diverse, urbane society and citizenry with competing and not uniform interests or moral codes.
- The idea of who the general reader is needs to account for the mature, adult reader stable in his or her beliefs and behavior.
- The marketplace functions as an adequate gatekeeper and protector of public tastes, with the publication, publicity, sales, and distribution apparatus ensuring that the legitimate publishing business will maintain decent standards, while under-the-counter smut and pornography will be kept marginal.
- The literary reputations of the author, the publisher, the reviewers, and the systems of literary review are legitimate, and can and should be invoked as evidence of quality and importance.
- Compared to pornography, the producers of which are anonymous, the books under consideration operate in a very different market. Pornography is for profit only with no other redeeming value, is sold under the counter, and without any kind of open exposure or review system in place.
- The courts should compare the book under examination with other books deemed acceptable by the courts.
- And, in modern life, books are just one among many influences of the modern media and entertainment industry (the press, the stage, movies), and to measure the harm of any given book is impossible.

These core elements of the Ernstian defense achieved considerable success in local and federal courts and became part of the standard repertoire for defending literary works against charges of obscenity, with Ernst a leading force in the progressive legal community on the eve of World War II. But other issues, and fissures in the progressive community, led Ernst away from a sustained focus on obscenity law. After the Nazi–Soviet Pact in August 1939, he turned his considerable energies to an ardent anti-communism, making his culturally progressive affiliations fraught, and his legacy within the ACLU controversial. Indeed, his obsession with communism and growing fealty to J. Edgar Hoover dominated Ernst's career by the early 1940s through the early 1950s, more than straining his relations with cultural and political progressives in general, and dimming his bright reputation over time, making him today a rather neglected figure.[29]

Friends and foes knew that Ernst was a dependable protector of Hoover and the FBI's reputation, although they did not know he had become a covert informant as well. Hoover assessed that he could rely on Ernst to do his bidding among the "responsible" and "serious liberal crowd,"[30] and Ernst became the pre-eminent liberal defender of the FBI, writing glowing tributes to Hoover and "his boys" in journals such as *The Nation,* and also in mainstream publications such as *Life, Saturday Evening Post,* and *Reader's Digest.*[31] The result for the civil liberties community was that a talented, well-respected leader spent his time promoting Hoover rather than challenging him. The result for Ernst was a diminution of his prestige and reputation within the community of civil libertarians among whom he had been a leader. He was never as influential after he became an active anti-communist as he had been before, and the irony is that by aligning himself with Hoover he wanted to be exceptionally influential. In the end, Morris Leopold Ernst made his mark in American literary and legal culture in the 1930s, while he was still a relatively young man, and he spent much of the rest of his career functioning not really as a champion of civil liberties, but rather as someone who once had been.

Notes

1. Conversation with Jonathan Rose, editor of *Book History.* The generalized arguments I make in this paper are based on reading thousands of documents in the Morris Ernst Collection in the Harry Ransom Humanities Center at the University of Texas, Austin (hereafter cited as MLE papers, HRC, followed by box and folder numbers). Specifically cited documents will be referred to in the text.

2. Among the many titles, those treating obscenity censorship matters in particular include the following: Morris L. Ernst and William Seagle, *To the Pure: A Study of Obscenity and the Censor* (New York: Viking Press, 1928); Morris L. Ernst and Alexander Lindey, *The Censor Marches On* (New York: Doubleday, Doran & Co., 1940); Morris L. Ernst, *The First Freedom* (New York: Macmillan, 1946); Morris L. Ernst and Alan U. Schwartz, *Censorship: The Search for the Obscene* (New York: Macmillan, 1964).

3. Radclyffe Hall, *The Well of Loneliness* (New York: Anchor/Doubleday, 1990 (originally published by Doubleday, 1928). For Ernst's records on the case, see MLE Papers,

HRC, vol. 90. The case tried by Ernst, *People v. Covici-Friede Inc., et al.,* was cleared in the court of Special Sessions, April 19, 1929. For additional records, see MLE files, HRC, box 740, folder 740.5, and HRC, box 383, folder 383.12. For treatment of the legal trials on *Well of Loneliness,* see Vera Brittain, *Radclyffe Hall: A Case of Obscenity?* (New York: A. S. Barnes and Company, 1968).

For Ernst's firm's correspondence and record of the legal materials surrounding the *Ulysses* case, see MLE files, HRC, vol. 93. The full Ernst firm documentation on the case can also be found in Michael Moscato and Leslie LeBlanc, eds., *Notes on the United States of America v. One Book Titled 'Ulysses' by James Joyce: Documents and Commentary—A 50-Year Retrospective* (Frederick, MD: University Publications of America, 1984). See Paul Vanderham, *James Joyce and the Censorship: The Trials of Ulysses* (New York: New York University Press, 1998).

4. Morrris L. Ernst and William Seagle, *To the Pure: A Study of Obscenity and the Censor* (New York: Viking Press, 1928; New York: Kaus Reprint Company, 1969). MLE papers, HRC, Vols. 90, 94–95 include most of the legal records surrounding the Magistrate Court cases, the New York State cases, and the Federal cases.

5. See David Rabban, *Free Speech in its Forgotten Years* (Cambridge: Cambridge University Press, 1997), especially for its treatment of Theodore Schroeder. See also Felice Flannery Lewis, *Literature, Obscenity & Law* (Carbondale: Southern Illinois University Press, 1976), for her treatment of literary obscenity trials prior to Ernst.

6. For a rich history of obscenity law and print culture, see Paul S. Boyer, *Purity in Print: Book Censorship in America from the Gilded Age to the Computer Age,* 2nd ed. (Madison: University of Wisconsin Press, 2002; 1st ed., 1968). Along with Boyer, two other scholars especially note Ernst's role in the obscenity law cases: Jay A. Gertzman, *Bookleggers and Smuthounds: The Trade in Erotica, 1920–1940* (University Park: University of Pennsylvania Press, 1999), who celebrates Ernst's role in the battles against the censors, and Rochelle Gurstein, *The Repeal of Reticence: America's Cultural and Legal Struggles over Free Speech, Obscenity, Sexual Liberation, and Modern Art* (New York: Hill and Wang, 1996), who is more critical in her estimation of the cultural legacy left by Ernst and other anti-censorship advocates.

7. For Ernst's work on sex hygiene and contraception matters, see HRC, MLE papers, vol. 90, and box 740, folder 740.5. On Ernst's relationship with Sanger, see Ellen Chesler, *A Woman of Valor: Margaret Sanger and the Birth Control Movement in America* (New York: Doubleday Anchor Books, 1992).

8. It might be noted here that Ernst did not succeed with this argument. To this day, the Supreme Court takes it for granted that the government does not need to prove "harm to minors" from sexual or vulgar material. There have been only two cases, to my knowledge, where lower federal courts have entertained such evidence: the *Eclipse* and *Playboy* cases. See Marjorie Heins's *Not in Front of the Children: Indecency, Censorship, and the Innocence of Youth* (New York: Hill and Wang, 2001), 135–36, 190–94.

9. My general framing of Ernst's arguments are distilled from the hundreds of documents, including trial briefs and appellate briefs in the literary obscenity cases, in HRC, MLE papers, especially vols. 90–94.

10. My overview of Ernst's relations with the ACLU are based on the hundreds of documents I have examined in the American Civil Liberties Union files at Princeton University, Seeley G. Mudd Library (hereafter cited as ACLU files, Princeton) and MLE papers, HRC. For discussion of Ernst's relations with Baldwin and the ACLU, see Robert C. Cottrell, *Roger Nash Baldwin and the American Civil Liberties Union* (New York: Columbia University Press, 2000); Samuel Walker, *In Defense of American Liberties: A History of the ACLU* (New York: Oxford University Press, 1991); and Alan Reitman, ed., *The Price*

of Liberty: Perspectives on Civil Liberties by Members of the ACLU (New York: W. W. Norton, 1968).

11. See Ernst, *Too Big* (Boston: Little, Brown & Co., 1940) for a full articulation of his anti-oligopoly position.

12. Thanks to Ernst and others, *Hicklin* was rejected in the Second Circuit Court of Appeals in the 1930s. But outside the Second Circuit, *Hicklin* remained the standard well into the 1950s. See Heins, *Not in Front of the Children,* 46.

13. Numerous scholars examine the *Hicklin* standard and its application in the American courts. For an excellent overview, see Heins, *Not in Front of the Children.* See also Frederick F. Schauer, *The Law of Obscenity* (Washington, DC: The Bureau of National Affairs, Inc., 1976), and Boyer, *Purity in Print.*

14. For an excellent treatment of the Comstock Act and contraceptive matters, and Comstock's public role in general, see Nicola Beisel, *Imperiled Innocents: Anthony Comstock and Family Reproduction in Victorian America* (Princeton: Princeton University Press, 1997), and Helen Lefkowitz Horowitz, *Rereading Sex: Battles Over Sexual Knowledge and Suppression in Nineteenth Century America* (New York: Knopf, 2002).

15. In *U.S. v. Harmon,* 1892, the Comstock Act was challenged on constitutional grounds, namely, that it interfered with First Amendment rights. But the federal court held that it was obvious that the First Amendment did not protect that which "outrages the common sense of decency, or endangers public safety." On *Harmon,* see Heins, *Not in Front of the Children,* and Schauer, *The Law of Obscenity.*

16. For an excellent treatment of the vulnerable-audience question in obscenity law, see Andrea Friedman, *Prurient Interests: Gender, Democracy, and Obscenity in New York City, 1909–1945* (New York: Columbia University Press, 2000); see also Heins, *Not in Front of the Children.*

17. *U.S. v. "What Happens"* documents are in HRC, MLE papers, vol. 90.

18. Ernst and Seagle, *To the Pure.* Ernst's battles with Sumner are documented throughout his papers, including the extensive records of the literary censorship trials in volumes 90–94.

19. See Boyer, *Purity in Print;* Gertzman, *Bookleggers and Smuthounds;* and Lewis, *Literature, Obscenity & Law.* See also Lewis Gannett's column, "Book and Things," *New York Herald,* December 29, 1933.

20. For a fuller study of Sumner's raids on New York City booksellers, see Gertzman, *Bookleggers and Smuthounds.*

21. Volumes 90, 94–95 of the MLE papers, HRC, have the complete legal record of these cases. For some correspondence about them, see MLE papers, box 740, folder 740.5. Other Magistrates Court cases Ernst defended against Sumner (and not always successfully) include Donald Henderson Clark's *Female;* Nathan Asch's *PayDay;* Clement Wood's *Flesh;* and Octave Mirbeau's *Celestine.*

22. Gannett, "Books and Things," *New York Herald,* December 29, 1933.

23. Ernst's draft of conclusion to appellant brief, n.d., box 47, folder 47.10)

24. The records for *U.S. v. Mary Ware Dennett,* 29 Fed (2d) 564 [1930] can be found in MLE papers, HRC, Vol. 86. For a full treatment of the Dennett case, see Constance M. Chen, *'The Sex Side of Life': Mary Ware Dennett's Pioneering Battle for Birth Control and Sex Education* (New York: New Press, 1996). See also Leigh Ann Wheeler, *Against Obscenity: Reform and the Politics of Womanhood in America, 1873–1935* (Baltimore: Johns Hopkins University Press, 2007).

25. *U.S. v. One Book Entitled 'Contraception,'* 51 F (2) 525, and *U.S. v. One Book Entitled 'Married Love,'* (48 Fed (2d) 821). MLE papers, Vol. 90 , and box 740, folder 740.5.

26. On the Ernst–Sanger relationship, see Chessler, *A Woman of Valor.*

27. The key birth-control cases that Ernst won in the federal courts include *United States v. One Package of Japanese Pessaries*, 86 Fed (2) 737; and *U.S. v. John P. Nicholas and U.S. v. Norman E. Himes*, (97 Fed (2) 510).

28. For Ernst's resounding declaration that these were the implications of these cases, see Ernst to BCFA, 3/30/39, HRC, MLE papers, Box 363, folder 363.1. He wrote: "As you know, two Federal Circuit courts of Appeal have held in language so clear as to permit no misconstruction that the prohibitions of the Federal contraception laws *do not apply* to physicians in their legitimate efforts to save life and protect health, nor to the druggists who act as the physicians' source of support. . . . These decisions have been accepted by law by the only departments in the Federal Government that have anything to do with prosecutions for violation of the laws in question, and *these departments operate on a nation-wide basis*" [Ernst's emphasis].

When the Attorney General, the chief law enforcement official of the United States, refused to ask the Supreme Court to review the decision in the *One Package* case, in effect he conceded its correctness and undertook to be bound by it. "We have been informed by counsel for the Post Office, both here in New York and in Washington, that the Post Office authorities consider legal the distribution by mail of contraceptive information and supplies when addressed to doctors and druggists. . . . I need scarcely point out that these rulings of executive department are not local matters confined to a particular circuit, but on the contrary reflect the existing national pattern." Box 363, folder 363.1.

29. For one of his studies of communism in the United States, see Morris L. Ernst and David Loth, *Report on the American Communist* (New York: Henry Holt and Company, 1952).

30. Ernst's FBI files, a nearly 1,000-page file available through the Freedom of Information Act/Privacy Acts Section, FBI File number 94-4-5366, are a fascinating body of documents indicating Ernst's willingness to aid Hoover's purposes. For an excellent treatment of this correspondence, see Harrison Salisbury, "The Strange Correspondence of Morris Ernst & John Edgar Hoover, 1939–1964," *The Nation*, December 1, 1984, 575–89.

Ernst's published writings from the 1940s through the 1960s, and the long private/ professional relationship with Hoover, reveal that Ernst became a dependable protector of Hoover and the FBI's reputation, and a surreptitious informant as well. The two most complete folders of Ernst–Hoover correspondence in the MLE papers, HRC, are in Box 99, folders 1 and 2: "J. Edgar Hoover & MLE 1/2/47–6/28/50, misc. corresp., RE: wiretapping, RE: loyalty program, etc." Many other boxes hold some correspondence.

31. See Ellen Schrecker, *Many Are the Crimes: McCarthyism in America* (Boston: Little, Brown and Company, 1998) for a wider-ranging examination of Ernst's role within the world of anti-communism.

PART THREE

The Limits of Liberalism

Sex/Body/Self

A Performance and Rant for the
Obscenity Conference

*The lights go out and Tim appears in a bright, whore-red follow spot completely
naked perched on a ledge.*

My body is a map. My body is a TEXT. My body is a STORY!
My body is a container for feeling and memory! My body is a HONEY-
　　　BAKED HAM!
NOOO! My skin is a map.
I am perched here naked on a precipice.

My skin is a map.
A map of my world. My secret world.
It tells you where I've been. And how to get to where I come from.
It charts my seas . . .
my caves . . .
my mountains. Such as they are!
my peninsulas . . .
PEN-INSULA! which from my semester of college Latin with a de-
　　　frocked priest I know means "almost-island."

I travel with this map over my skin.

I go on journeys. Find new coastlines. Hidden borders.
I follow my nose along the touch that has pulled me through life.
I lead with my tongue.
I go by foot . . . by dick . . . by brain sometimes.
I know the path by heart.
The pleasures I sailed across.
The pain I pointed towards.
The knowing my bends and hollows.
The bodies . . . many bodies . . . I have touched and been taught by.
The secret places soothed and stroked.
My skin is a map.

Tim begins to walk nude among the obscenity conference attendees, thus earning his honorarium.

Well that is not really true. My skin is not a map. My skin is what tends to get me in trouble and then we can map that trouble all over the world. Like when I was performing in Tokyo and I walked naked among the audience of 400: a big foreign fag *gaijin* naked man. I had never felt more naked as I gamboled without clothes through the aisles in Japan and came near a Dokkyo University student whose gaze crept further and further inside her armpit. Now admittedly, I have made young ladies—as well as young men—all over the English-speaking world shrink into their seats with eyes gazing heavenward when they encounter my queer narratives on stage and even queerer naked body in the orchestra seats.

Or the time in Durham, NC, a few years back. I was on the cover of a North Carolina newspaper *The Independent.* In the photograph I am almost naked with Senator Jesse Helms leering like a vampire behind me. This festive image brought out hundreds of right-wing protesters to my performances to try to stop my show in Durham. There was one small girl carrying a sign in the protest outside the theater that says, "YECHH! TIM MILLER KEEP YOUR CLOTHES ON!" I am so stressed by the protests that I am forced to pick up an audience member, a gorgeous black PhD student from UNC Chapel Hill. After the show, he and I shoved our way thru the protesters, went to my hotel and fucked one another in a marathon session to try to make us feel better about Amerika. It worked!

All those dry cleaning bills audience members all over the world sent to me when I sat my naked sweaty butt on their Sunday best and left a butt imprint, a kind of living booty shroud of Turin!

So you see my skin is not a map. My skin—especially my naked skin—is a trouble spot. It's a place where I always get messed up. It's a place where the police get called. It's a place where I will never get tenure.

Tim steps onstage.

My skin is all of those things. That why I want to start.

Tim puts his clothes on. Follow spot blazingly bright white.

Let's start at the beginning. The very beginning. My Dad is fucking my Mom. In a bed. Where else would they be? This is suburban Whittier, California. They're young and hot for each other. I'm trying to visualize this. Half of me is inside my Father's dick. The other half is inside my Mom. My biology gets a little vague here. They're breathing fast. My Dad is going to cum any minute. He's thrusting madly. AH AH AH! Suddenly I am thrown out of my Father's dick into my Mom's body. I am surrounded by thousands of squirming creatures.

I am swimming upstream.
Oh humble dog paddle!
Oh efficient crawl!
Oh stylish backstroke!

I am swimming upstream. As I would swim upstream throughout this life. One queer little spermlet . . . Fighting the odds. A hideous sperm that looks like Senator Jesse Helms tries to catch me in a net. I elude him! There's a bunch of generals from the Joint Chiefs of Staff who want to kick me and all the other gay sperm out of this fallopian tube. I elude them, as well. Then a bunch of hulking macho slimebag straight-pig sperm shove and try to elbow me out of the way. Call me "Sissy! Pansy! Fag!

You'll never find an egg! HA HA HA!"

Clearly this is homophobia. My very first experience. But! I use my superior agility, fleetness, and sense of style and calmly leap from plodding straight sperm forehead to straight sperm forehead. I quickly find a willing dyke ovum, we agree to power share. We reach consensus immediately (this is a fantasy sequence, all right!) and we . . .

FERTILIZE!

There is an explosion of creative electricity. A shifting of queer tectonic plates.

Skittering across the well of loneliness to Walt Whitman's two boys together clinging on the sea beach dancing! I see Gertrude Stein is in a tutu. She dances with Vaslav Nijinsky in a butt plug. They do a Pas de Deux on the wings of a fabulous flying machine created by Leonardo and piloted by James Baldwin and Amelia Earhart. They fly over the island of Lesbos where Sappho is starting to put the moves on the cute woman carpenter who had arrived to build her a breakfast nook.

There is a puff of feathers . . . an angry fist . . . a surface to air witticism. . . . the off the shoulder amazon look! Embodying the bridge between woman and man and back again. The sperm is a fish. The egg is a rocket. 5, 4, 3, 2, 1!

And . . . ECCE HOMO! Behold the fag.

And now the big cry to the universe. It's time to be born. WAAAAHH!

The doctor spanks my butt. WAAAHH! He spanks it again. WAAAHH! I look back and I say

"Doctor, I won't really be into spanking till I'm a Freshman in College!"

With that first pre-erotic and non-consensual spank a wave of shame and body fear washes over me. I fight back. I kick the doctor in the balls. Rejecting his authority. I slip on my "Action = Life" Huggies. Slither into my attractive "We're Here We're Queer Get Used To It" powder-blue baby jumper. I see all the other queer babies in the nursery start to shimmer and grow and explode from their diapers. We all grow to adulthood. So many of them find their way to the University of Iowa Obscenity Conference tonight.

Until I stand before you now.

Tim bows. Applause! Grabs the microphone.

I'm going to perform several pieces for my presentation, but I want to also use my time to blur the boundaries between the performer-self and the holding-forth-in-another-way self. I'd like to talk a little more in terms of this obscenity conference and my performances and the enormous role that this particular subject has played in my work. So I'll talk a little bit between each of the pieces. And one thing for me that is very important is to really acknowledge what makes each of us tick, what influences and emboldens us to create work. And for me especially in terms of my own difficulties with the U.S. government, not just around the first amendment or the National Endowment for the Arts, but all of the many ways I feel my government assaults my personhood, my home, my family. Certainly my first amendment battles are one of the big pieces of that, but I don't think any of this space claiming, or any of my naked wandering through the audience imagining new and more efficient strategies of overthrowing the Bush administration, would have ever occurred to me without a few crucial influences. My work is totally informed and encouraged by all of the feminist performance work I saw growing up in the late 1970s in Los Angeles at the "Women's Building" in downtown L.A. where I was seeing as a teen this explosion of feminist performance practice of people really claiming the narratives of our bodies, the particulars of our daily lives, what counts, what matters to us, our dreamscapes, certainly also our queer selves. It encouraged my agency as a little queer boy and also made me want to be a lesbian when I grew up. And I've done my best—I think I'm going to write a little fantasy piece where I was raised by lesbian wolves in the Hollywood Hills—I've been watching HBO's mini-series *Rome* too much . . .

Anyway, there was just this sense at that time in Southern California that "Okay, this is my life, the personal is political." This was a crucial inscription on my body and the texts that live within as I launched into the world. Of course, sticking my metal fork in the electrical socket of the "personal is political" circuitry has contributed endlessly to my getting in trouble—getting strange confederate flags waved outside my shows and homophobic death threats from time to time. It was a huge gift to me from feminism: to imagine that my queer boy's life, desires, and narratives mattered.

Second, I was also for a short time in a terrible punk rock band with my boyfriend in High School—the worst imaginable punk rock band— we had only two of the three chords we needed to do our specialty songs built around the texts of the Marquis de Sade. The great thing was that we had never even read the Marquis de Sade. Terrible punk posturing aside, this gave me an incredible set of tools to add into all the Marxist-feminist-lesbian new ways to understand the world. I knew I had to jump on the table, annoy the neighbors, get the cops called, raise your voice loud with punk chord progressions.

Finally for me was coming of age in high school during an explosion of lesbian and gay civil rights in California—which certainly in the late 1970s was where "the action" was in almost every way. With the election of Harvey Milk as the first openly gay male elected official in the United States, I knew I needed to connect my personal identity as a gay man with political praxis. Harvey Milk took office and was there for a short time before a right-wing cop blew his brains out in one of the more successful political coups in American history—though we've had many more successful ones of late. So somehow that swirl of influences of the Feminism, Punk Rock, and Gay Civil Rights is always with me whenever my work is problematized or tarred with the obscenity brush and I get some nutty Congressman Bob Dornan on the floor of the United States House of Representatives in open debate calling me a "porno-slime jerk"—which my mom happened to see on C-Span while she was on her treadmill watching TV: "Honey, you were just called a 'porno-slime jerk' in the U.S. House of Representatives." I like acknowledging those influences because I think they're core to what I do. And certainly my own formula here is mirrored by many other artists who started making work in the juicy ferment of the eighties in response to the craziness of that Reagan-Bush era where all kinds of voices were being claimed—new strategies: sexuality, politics, community identification. Suddenly all of this work coming out of queer communities, communities of color, disabled folks' performance work. One of my proudest accomplishments is founding the two main centers for on-the-edge performance work: PS 122 in New York and Highways Performance Space in Los Angeles. At Highways we were doing a festival of performance coming from the Asian Pacific Islander communities and we were presenting a storyteller from the leper colony in Hawaii (he has a book out, it's quite amazing). Anyway, the most untouchable, the most cast out in the Western cultural matrix, is of course the leper. "I've got to have a leper at Highways in Santa Monica!" And that his shows delighted and troubled the sold-out audiences gave me a real sign of hope that the franchise is widening, that more and more voices were adding their stories, politics, and erotics.

So out of that space it's not so surprising that this work, and hopefully mine included, got fiercer, got funnier, was gathering larger audiences, was getting more press, was showing up in major media in Chattanooga of all things, or—like this piece I just performed now about the queer sperm—on an episode of the HBO show "The Larry Sanders Show" which was built around me coming on and doing that piece—mentioning a "butt-plug" was "the problem" on the HBO segment called "The Performance Artist"—so out of all that as this work got stronger and more connected to who we are and how we relate to the world as artists, it's not surprising that the Reagan-Bush junta started to bash back. And certainly in 1990 when myself, Karen Finley, Holly Hughes, and John Fleck became the so-called "National Endowment for the Arts Four," the "NEA Four." This was not the first example of being embattled because I had been going through eight years already of the homophobic inaction of the Reagan–Bush administration allowing eighty thousand Americans to die before Reagan deigned to say the word AIDS and I was regularly being arrested with the AIDS Coalition to Unleash Power (ACT UP) as we protested with fierce creative flair. The culture war did open up a new front, a new space, where my work in a way really got twisted and tortured in a way that really surprised me. I'm such a Pollyanna and embarrassingly so full of white privilege that I actually believed way too much in what I learned with my "A" in Civics class. I actually imagined that the "separation of powers" would never let President Bush mess with the NEA, that gay people would someday be treated like citizens and that the First Amendment protected creative expression—all those things that I've mostly disabused myself of since— I actually couldn't imagine that I could live in a country where oppositional, queer artists like me would not be encouraged, nurtured with a tiny little bit of our tax money.

So out of this juicy period in which I was as likely to be performing at "Actors Theater of Louisville" or the "Brooklyn Academy of Music" as I was to be collaborating with an Episcopalian priest doing performance art sermons or collaborating with Guillermo Gomez-Pena at the Central American Cultural Center in Los Angeles around the huge wound in my state, well in our whole country, around immigration and the bicultural reality of a North American country that speaks two primary languages, English and Spanish. The "personal is political" formation means that our lives as artists and citizens are constantly being engaged and challenged.

So that's a little bit of setting-up-the-scene, but I think it's time for another performance. I think one of the huge sustaining things to come out of all of those teenage, queer-boy, wish-I-was-a-lesbian evenings at the "Women's Building" in downtown L.A. was this real interest in exploring the narratives that live in our bodies and the myths, the memories, and the meanings that live in our assholes, and our elbows, and our pancreases—pancrei or whatever you call them!—and that's a real ongoing teaching exploration for me. I was just here a few months ago at the U of I working with some MFA actors and playwrights and we did some explorations of narratives that live in our bodies and people produced some really powerful and charged stuff. So I want to do a little piece jumping out of that.

Tim is caught in a followspot as the stage goes dark and walks slowly into audience.

My hands . . . my hands . . .
My hands have been slapped a lot in my life.

Tim takes an audience member's hand in his and regards their palm.

Most people think you learn about someone by reading the palm of the hand, but I think we can learn just as much from the back of our hands. You just need to be able to see the echo, the imprint of the times that that person's hand has been slapped.

My hand got slapped when I reached my hand in the cookie jar for just one more.

My hand got slapped when my first boyfriend was queer-bashed when I was eighteen. He had gone to a different High School than I did. They yelled at him "Die Faggot Die" as they stabbed him nine times in the neck with an ice pick outside of a gay bar in Garden Grove, CA.

My hand got slapped when certain right-wing Congressmen said that no lesbian or gay artists should be able to raise their voice in America.

My hand got slapped very hard in Fifth Grade when I cut holes in the pocket of my pants. Neat Virgo holes here in my faggy maroon cords. I did this for a good reason so I could put my Fifth Grade fingers through those holes and touch my Fifth Grade Dick and balls during English lessons, subject-verb agreement. Now, this didn't hurt my command of the English language. I speak English very well. I have written a book. I'm a professor. My mom discovered my shame when she was hanging the washing up in the backyard to dry on the clothesline.

She discovered the holes when she pulled the pockets inside out to dry better in the sun. She slapped my hands and said to me "Don't fiddle! Don't fiddle! Don't fiddle!"

FIDDLE? I am always getting caught, caught red-handed.

Tim heads back onto the stage which floods with bright as noon Montana sunlight.

We're here in Montana. Bozeman, Montana. It's 1997 Lesbian and Gay Pride in the State of Montana. BIG SKY PRIDE! I am here to perform for Montana Pride. Montana is a big state, about the size of Western Europe, so people have to drive for twelve hours to get to Pride in Bozeman. There are about eight or nine hundred Lesbians and Gay men from around the state here. There are also about eight or nine hundred other people here to celebrate Gay Pride. Montana Militia had sent a bunch of folks. This was their fifteen minutes of fame what with the FBI standoff that summer. The KKK has representatives from twelve counties in Wyoming, Montana, and Idaho. The White Aryan Nation has sent two busloads from Coeur D'Alene. We're all one big happy family here in America and we're all together to enjoy Montana Lesbian and Gay Pride. There are more pick-up trucks with gun racks in the back than I have ever seen in my entire life. Unfortunately not one of them belongs to a butch dyke. I personally believe that lesbians are the only people who should be allowed to possess firearms in America. This is my version of gun control. It's been tense here, bomb threats, Montana State Police with telescopic rifles on the roofs of buildings on Main Street as we marched. This is one of those gigs I do in America, like in Chattanooga, where the police warn me for my safety to never stand in front of windows while the protesters wave their confederate flags as the audience arrives for the show.

I am walking to a Lesbian and Gay Wedding in Bozeman, Montana. I have done my performance the night before and now I'm going to take part in the last event of Pride weekend.

I am walking across a street in Bozeman on the way to the wedding and I can feel Alistair's hand in mine, his long cool fingers woven with mine. We've been through a lot in the last years. We're doing pretty good in 1997. We've gotten so much closer. Dealt with shit, I say "I love you" now without any rehearsal required. Everything is pretty good except for one thing. Alistair is not here with me. No Yellowstone vacation for us. Alistair is on the other side of the world being told by my government that he is not welcome here. He does not get to be in Montana holding the hand of his lover, boyfriend, husband, partner, I don't care what you call us. The U.S. Consulate won't let him in to the States, has rejected his student visa, his return ticket is no good now, and he has had to drop out of University because he's missed the beginning of the term and our lives are falling apart thanks to the U.S. government and I am walking across a street in Bozeman, Montana.

Two men in a pick-up with a gun rack in the back window pull up and stop next to me. I know what's coming. I don't have to call the psychic friends network. What's coming is so predictable. What's coming are "F's."

Fucking.
Faggot.
Fruit.
Fairy.
Freak.

They're predictable, but they're scary too, like an angry dog straining at its leash. I know that those F's were usually followed by something more concrete, a rock, a bottle, maybe even a piece of concrete. Sure enough, a half-empty or, depending on your worldview, half-full bottle of Colt 45 Malt Liquor leaves the passenger side window as it's flung at me. This was not an individual serving, this was a Sunday morning family-size bottle of Colt 45. It flew through the air, its geometry perfect, I could admire it for a moment even under these circumstances as it made a graceful arc and hit me direct on my right hand. My red, red hand—redder now from the hot blood dripping down my fingers. The bottle bounced and shattered at my feet. It's not too bad, five or six stitches tops, I just hope the guns stay in the gun rack.

I would like to say that at this moment I became homo superhero. I would tear off my clothes and instead of my vulnerable naked flesh, there would be an ugly superhero unitard costume. I would jump on the cab of their truck, kick the windshield in, and drag these two assholes across the broken glass. But I didn't do any of those things. I'm not strong enough, or dumb enough, to do that. I wish I could be like my friend Mark in Iowa City. When someone yells "FAGGOT!" at him on the street, he has a commitment to immediately drop his pants and underwear, turning his back to them, spreading his butt cheeks and shouting, "Yeah, I am a big faggot. Why don't you come here and lick my pussy!" I just can't do that. I guess I just don't have that spirit of Iowa in me. I just bowed my head and walked quicker, a deer frozen in the oncoming headlights. Well, the light changed and the men in the truck lost interest in me. They threw one or two more F's and then went on their way. I rubbed the blood, and the growing green and purple and red on my hand, my hand which just a moment before had been holding Alistair's. His hand slips into mine and the world goes mad. It's almost like they could see Alistair's hand in mine. It's not enough that our country has tried to destroy our relationship, these men in the truck still want to stick our hands in the frying pan, hold our hands to the flame as I cross a beautiful street in Montana made ugly by these men's hate.

Well, I wasn't much in the mood for going to a wedding now, but what else could I do. So off I went.

My hand aching for the absence of Alistair's hand in mine.

My head aching from the harsh ricochet of those F's.

My heart aching for these dozen lesbian and gay couples getting ready to bind their lives in an old school gymnasium in Bozeman, Montana.

I'm really interested in all of the ways these terrains, these borders of our identity and selfhood in a way get thrown into the kind of crazy toxic soup—not just in this country but this is where we are so it's our problem—this crazy American homophobic alphabet soup. The eight years I spent around the NEA material, taking a case to the U.S. Supreme Court, got added into the mix of past letters like HIV and AIDS which transformed my sense of what it is to be an artist, an activist, part of a community in this country. New letters have been added these last years thanks to the INS (now known as ICE, Immigration and Customs Enforcement). The struggles I've been going through for the last thirteen years now with my Australian-Scottish partner to try to keep him in this country as his final visa winds down is now part of that soup that I keep having to dive into every morning I wake up in this America that limits artists' agency in a way around those letters N.E.A., I.N.S., H.I.V., A.I.D.S. And that soup, as it simmers away as I travel all over the country—thirty states every year—and perform, I really like engaging these issues. And certainly in the last few years I've been focused much more around this larger limiting of agency and freedom of expression of thirty million gay people around the culture-war battle about civil marriage equality, which is certainly a huge surprising space that many years ago I might not have thought I'd be spending so much of my rhetorical flourishes and activism and performance-opining to be addressing. But, like it or not, it's probably the front line of the culture war right now and what cynically gets used to try to bash gay people in Ohio to sleaze out another shoddy victory in that state that decided the last election.

So as I travel and talk about stuff just like I am now or perform a full piece or go perform at a state university in Tennessee and talk in some ways and perform just like I am now for a class visit at some intro contemporary society general requirement class. There's a couple of hundred people in a lecture hall—and I know suddenly maybe some of those people, and not just in Tennessee or in Montana or in the suburban conservative parts of my own state—I know frequently they've just never had someone that naughty, naked, political, queer, in a position of authority in a classroom or in a theater. And again and again, after I do a presentation to a class or a performance someone who I would clearly profile as a straight, white, Republican, Baptist, home-schooled, lacrosse-playing, frat boy will come and present himself to me: "Ya know, Tim, I'm a straight, white, Republican, Baptist, home-schooled, lacrosse-playing, frat boy"—"Really?!"—we all play our parts—"And I don't know if you and Alistair should be able to get married, but I think you should have all the rights of a straight couple." And you know so for me that's the space and that's where the work is I'm really interested in doing within the culture wars, where we hit the jackpot like that in what that young man said to me. It was like the three red cherries lined up, you know ching-ching-ching, bells-and-whistles, the jack-pot happens, the light-bulb going on. The treasure of what this country might some-day become pours at our feet.

These battles around content, obscenity, have hounded me for a number of years. Regularly there would be protests outside my shows or people would be losing their jobs or funding because they presented me, which made me feel very guilty. I want to focus on one incident not that long ago in 1999, when I was performing in Chattanooga for the first time. I probably perform in the southeast more than any other part of the country. I don't know, maybe the text of my work and the complexity of that Senator Helms from North Carolina has woven me in, in a strong way, to the fabric of the southeast. The south interests me a lot but it was the first time I'd performed in Chattanooga and there'd been an enormous amount of fuss on the front page of the Sunday paper. In my newest book from the University of Wisconsin there's an essay I'm very happy about called "The Battle of Chattanooga" (typical grandiose me) equating my little wars around culture with that big nasty Civil War and all the battle around Chattanooga in 1864. That civil war is ongoing of course. I'd been on the cover of the Sunday Chattanooga Times-Free Press, had already been on "Good Morning Chattanooga," and the headline was basically "OBSCENE FAG COMES TO CHATTANOOGA (Lock up the children)." A huge important thing happened there. It's not about me and my work being aggrandized, or inflated or puffed up, because actually what these moments where the sparks fly or where the shit hits the fan, as they've happened at this University as they happen everywhere from time to time, actually scare the shit out of me. What really matters is this amazing opportunity for change, for people to claim space. It actually has nothing to do with me. And every night there at "Barking Legs Theatre" on Dodds Avenue in Chattanooga as the audience made their way through the protest of these white supremacist north Georgia churches who had all made me the subject of their Sunday sermons after seeing the Sunday paper, waving their confederate flags and having their children scream at the audience, the real performance was not me performing, it was actually the audience arriving, choosing to park their car, walk through two blocks of shouting protesters. We were sold out for the run, the benefit of controversy, I'll admit it—*and every single ticket got picked up.* No one took a look at the right wing protesters and decided to head home. Chattanooga is an interesting and complex community—but also had been a very closeted city, and there hadn't really been a big highly visible queer thing like this with the amount of media I was getting—it actually gave people in that community a chance to see, not their neighbors, see these outside people who had come in, and Chattanooga is a city of jazz clubs and barbeque and you know, in the good old days, whore-houses, it was the New York for the Tennessee River area, a really charged and interesting space.

And it's a majority black city. So all of a sudden all these white people from north Georgia churches were coming and waving confederate flags, which is very provocative of course—yet another symbol we fight about in our discussions around the first amendment. The African American cops were very annoyed by these confederate flags on the streets. These were the police who were protecting the theater, the audience and me personally since there had been lots of very specific threats—to the point where I was advised to keep my head down in the car as I went home. One African American police officer in Chattanooga who I became quite friendly with over the four nights—on the last night of the show he told me sort of conspiratorially: "Ya know those cracker protesters, they're not parked illegally but I'm gonna go ticket 'em anyway for you." So it's the only time I've been all for the abuse of police powers. The heat on the street actually just gave a chance, and heat is generated around a naked body or a word or an image starts going and people can kind of freak out and start going all Mr. Smith on "Lost in Space" about it—but that heat creates a space where it's actually this tremendous opportunity for people to change, to recognize energies that are around us. Generally the last thing I want to do on the day I arrive at a college in North Carolina is to go spend five hours with the theater students and the "Campus Crusade for Christ" students to dialog about the conflicts that come from me performing on campus. On the other hand if you order a pizza there's the possibility that we'll all stay in the room together and talk to each other. And that's happened again and again in my journeys, which is something I'm extremely interested in—how do we create those little change moments, light bulb moments, walking through the protesters, looking them in the eye, shouting back, as those people did on Dodds Avenue in Tennessee.

Anything that keeps claiming our private identity, sure, but also how that heads out into the social sphere and makes tangible change happen. And oddly in some ways, that opportunity is created because I have been sometimes hassled as "porno-slime jerk," a critique which is so ridiculous since my work is so within an American, Chautauqua, solo-performance, avuncular public address, speech contest in high school form. (I admit it: I did Forensics Speech Contests! There's currently all these queer boys in Texas on YouTube who do my work in speech contests, which I'm writing an essay about because I find it so interesting that they're there in their bedrooms, doing my shows from my books, and winning their state competitions in Texas and Illinois with my queer material!)

On that note, I think it is a time for a homosexual orgy, don't you? I want to do one last piece and that'll be it for tonight. And I don't think I need to preface anything—no I guess I'll just dive into this. But I wanted to do this piece tonight, partly I'm really interested in this space of imagining from that heat of these battles that sometimes happen around our bodies, our cocks, our cunts, our hearts, our politics, that there actually is this huge possibility for change. And I was recently performing in Winston-Salem at Wake Forest, which is you know a big great University but also an affiliated Baptist college. And I was premiering my new show, "A Thousand and One Beds," and there is just this one part where I'm eighteen and I've just been fucked in the butt on Hollywood Boulevard and I've got cum dripping out of my butt onto the "Walk of Fame" on the John Travolta star, and before the show as I kneel down in prayer before I do the Lord's Work I thought "I really can't say this in Winston-Salem at Wake Forest University." But then of course I went ahead and with the students I was working with it was that moment afterwards—"Oh my god, that piece was so amazing, that part of it, it gives me courage in the piece we're working on in our project. I'm going to and talk about that."—so that's like, even in those moments where we doubt ourselves—the truth is every time I do that little particular section I get extremely embarrassed, although John Travolta always gets a laugh—so anyway I'll just dive into this piece.

Civil disobedience weekend performance

Tim picks up an electronic bullhorn and begins to harangue the audience.

"You're all about to be placed under arrest for OBSCENITY. You are here in violation of the Patriot Act. In violation of the Federal Law, National Endowment for Censorship Penal Code, yes Penal Code S-Q-143-Q. And the Lord Bush said 'Thou shalt not protest the U.S. government, make or view oppositional queer performance art with erotic transformative images of the future!' If you do not disperse immediately you will be placed under arrest. You are now under arrest! The charge is blocking a Federal Orifice! I mean Office!

"You are now under arrest! You are now under arrest! You are now under arrest!"

We linked arms and chanted furiously . . . STOP BUSH! FIGHT BACK! SAVE ART! END WAR! And for our bi-lingual number ALTO A LA CENSURA! Art is not a crime! Which the next day the newspapers would report as "Hola a la Censura." Ooops! We doffed our art criminal chain gang outfits and blockaded the Federal Building. Shutting that building down in protest of our Government's attacks on civil liberties, the 1st Amendment and Freedom of Expression. This was the big moment . . . the time where all our careful training . . . our split second organization . . . our carefully honed message . . . no more rehearsing or nursing a part . . . we were about to enter. . . .

CIVIL DISOBEDIENCE WEEKEND!

We stood there . . . Bicep to bicep . . . ego to ego . . . one by one the cops took us away . . . Les and Adrian and Tom and Guillermo and Jordan and Kathy. . . . Finally it was my turn . . . and I felt the cold steel of those federal handcuffs so tight . . . so very tight around my wrists . . . so deliciously tight . . . and they lined us up underneath a picture of George Bush. Our hands handcuffed behind us . . . in the perfect position to grab the crotch of the person behind . . . and then they marched us off and put the guys in one holding tank and the women in another.

We sat there. One of the federal cops said to us . . ."You can communicate with each other all you want . . . but NO TALKING!"

They processed our paperwork. It was like we were checking into a hotel. There were bunk beds as far as I could see in this holding cell. There must have been 1001 BEDS. Why does the US have so much space to lock people up? The Federal Cop came in and said, Well, I see we got 24 real ARTFAGS in here. Well boys, since you got arrested so late on this Friday, the Federal Judge has already gone home. We're gonna keep you here all weekend! We protested . . . but our dogs, our jobs, our boyfriends! The Federal Cop just gave us a cold stare and said . . .

TOUGH LUCK BOYS, WELCOME TO CIVIL DISOBEDIENCE WEEKEND!

We resigned ourselves to our fate and we began to talk together in groups of two and three. Then the highly sexy Jose went to the toilet, unzipped his pants, pulled out his dick, and took a piss. A strange and horrible realization dawned that this was a very cute bunch of Civil Disobedience Dudes locked in a holding tank for the weekend with nothing to do . . . no copy of "Remembrances of Things Past" to sooth those long hours. No Pictionary Set! No laptops! What could we possibly do?

I was sitting next to the cute semiotics instructor from Cal-Arts who started rubbing something in his pants. It was not a book by Michel Foucault. It was not chopped liver. It was the beginning of

CIVIL DISOBEDIENCE WEEKEND!

He said, "Boy, these anti-Bush civil disobedience anti-censorship actions sure get me all hot."

I said, "Yeah. Me too."

He said "Hey, I'm really stiff. Getting tenure was a bitch. How about a back rub?"

I said, "Sure, Dude." All eyes were on us. Hands begin to move underneath "MOVEON.ORG" T-Shirts and that message took on whole new meaning. Now, Tom, who was a lighting designer at several performance spaces around town, found that this holding cell came conveniently equipped with several household dimmers and he quickly made the mood a little more ambient.

A trembly, pregnant, and luscious apprehension suffused the room . . . that dank and drear holding tank. The Olympic Anthem theme song snuck in through the ventilation shaft . . . One of the boys from Highways reached into the pants of one of the boys from the LA County Museum of Art and they began to kiss big wet sloppy larger than life tongue kissing. Like the kind you see on late night TV Mexican Telenovellas. Like the kind you read about in repressed Edwardian gay private Diaries. Like the kind I practiced on a towel the night before I took my girlfriend to Disneyland in 8th Grade and we made out on the "Journey to Inner Space Ride." Those kinds of kisses.

The semiotics instructor from Cal Arts has now pulled his dick out and is demonstrating the Theory of Signification to the Graduate Student from the Inland Empire . . . the pants are dropping . . . shirts are pulled over heads in a practical arabesque . . . generally stroking and soothing and generally fulfilling our foray.

Though the state may chain us . . . our crazed and juicy bodies and imaginations will not be imprisoned . . .

> *"With love's light wings did I o'erperch these walls,*
> *For stony limits cannot hold love out:*
> *And what love can do, that dares love attempt."*

And this is our revolt . . . our disobedience most uncivil here in the bowels of George Bush's Federal Building we will whip 'em out and come on his hideous Bushy smirk and fake cowboy hat . . . wipe it on his WMD dossier of lies that lead us into this war that will kill a million people before it's done . . . naked together on a burning flag in North Carolina . . . raising high the roofbeam, the standard and anything else that's handy including the sleeveless T-shirt stretched so tastefully behind the neck of the blond boy with the lovely butt who comes from the Simi Valley Anti-Censorship and Homo-phile Auxiliary who is being tended to by the People for the American Way Outreach co-coordinator who is in fact reaching out, from behind, pinching his nipples . . . while the Events Coordinator from the National Campaign for Freedom of Expression is licking his balls while, with an excruciatingly slow up and down motion, is jacking on his activist member. I remain distant . . . observant . . . my job is to stay aware of what is going on . . . so it can be written down . . . it must be written . . . it must be saved . . . this part of ourselves . . . the jump off point . . . ready to speak truth to Caesar *and* jerk off on his best toga . . . or, if not on his best toga, at least in his sandal in the middle of the night so that the next day as he divides Gaul his foot goes squish squish and he slips and falls and hits his head before he invades another country.

Everyone is in on the act now. THERE ON THE 1001 BEDS IN THE HOLDING CELL! It is a flurry of safer activist sex! I am writing furiously . . . there is more than I can describe . . . the hand does not move fast enough. Skin is slapping . . . thighs are clenching. . . . breath is racing. One after another we come on the face of George Bush. On a banner with the words GUILTY burned across his forehead. He is now awash in the semen of 24 pissed off artist fags . . . defiant even in the slammer . . . the joint . . . the big house . . . saying NO to anti-gay, anti-peace, anti-free speech fascists!

We all cum and fall on each other spent. But, then, we hear footsteps . . . voices . . . then hundreds of people rush into the basement of the Federal Building with a confused shout. We are being released!

We meet the women as they are let out of their holding cell. They have used their time in custody to form a Lesbian Video Collective! How do they do these things? We shot a load. They founded an arts organization! They have already shot their first feature! Amazing. It's a remake of the classic *Maedchen in Uniform,* which they have sensibly retitled for English distribution *Pussy Come Home!*

WHAT HAS HAPPENED? WE MAKE OUR WAY OUT TO THE STREET.

We hear the haunting strains of the ending of Beethoven's 9th Symphony.

Now, out on the streets, there is strange music in the air.

There are thousands of people dancing in the streets. Carrying garlands of flowers and speaking dozens of languages. Alistair runs to greet me and takes my hand. People of every cultural and community background have taken the street in front of the Federal Building. The LA Philharmonic has come down from the Hollywood Bowl for an impromptu celebratory playing of Beethoven's 9th there on the nearly liberated Civic Center Mall.

> *Seid umschlungen . . . Millionen . . . Diesen Kuss der ganzen Welt!*
> Be embraced . . . ye millions . . . this kiss for all the world!

We begin to hear snippets of what has happened. George Bush has been IMPEACHED and is FACING A WAR CRIMES TRIAL IN BAGDHAD? HMMM.

The new president has appointed Holly Hughes head of the NEA?

The Federal Police have given up and joined our cause? HMMM.

Dick Cheney has given up hunting and has come out as a gay person? YEEECHHH! Oh please God, anything but that.

And most mysterious of all . . . there are confirmed reports that numerous historical monuments all over this country have transubstantiated! No longer are they monuments to war but now honor those who fought for social justice and against Neo-Fascist censorship during these long dark years.

There is dancing and music . . . fireworks in the air. We hear more. A fax from Washington tells us that the new Congress has elevated the AIDS Crisis and homophobia to the highest National Priority. The Supreme Court has upheld that marriage equality for gay folks is a Constitutional right. A telegram arrives from UN Security Council. They want to meet with us immediately to form a world artists' government to address nuclear disarmament . . . economic restructuring . . . global warming. The nation has been moved by our deeds! We have triumphed! The day is ours!

I think of the work left to be done and I glance up at the top of the Federal Building. The cold concrete façade is finally cracking open and sprouting strange and beautiful vines, tendrilling into the night . . . testament to the seeds planted on this Civil Disobedience Weekend.

Those vines are growing up and they are rooting deep . . . growing towards something new.

Towards something that if we all put in a lot of vision . . .
a little imagination . . . and tons of work.
They're growing towards what just might . . .
What just might be . . .

. . . our future.

Tim and Beethoven's 9th climax. Simultaneously. It's a fantasy, okay?

I just want to say just before we end the conference for tonight that it is an interesting and charged moment we are in. This piece that I just performed—I've been performing it for the last year—and for the first few months I was doing it I thought "Man, Tim you are such a fucking Pollyanna." And of late, these last months, it's starting to feel like that vision, that possibility of change is feeling much more alive. I was here in Iowa City on election night, November 8th, 2006, and I remember we were at the Vitro Hotel with the Democratic Party of Johnson County and it was one of the most joyous experiences of my life. I don't know if it was quite as good as a gay sex orgy in federal detention that overthrows the Bush Administration, but it was close! In these interesting times, I just want to encourage everybody to dive in and take a big bite out of this moment we're living through. Stuff in America is shifting and changing and we just need to, as our dear departed Allen Ginsberg would say, "Keep our queer shoulders to the wheel."

Forging Hetero-Collectives

Obscenity Law in India

On matters of obscenity in India, the law stages more than the now-familiar tussle between censorship and freedom of expression. Sections 292–294 of the Indian Penal Code (IPC) codify obscenity within the law. Introduced by British colonial order in the 1860s, these laws have been revised and expanded since, and have been supplemented with the landmark Indecent Representation of Women Act (Prohibition) of 1986–87. Sections 292–294 deem representations to be obscene if they are lascivious, prurient, indecent, and corrupt or if they cause depravity. Obscenity is understood not only as lust and lewdness but also as a contagion of sexual depravity. Indeed, the law codifies obscenity as a metonym for the excesses of sexuality. The leading cultural metaphor for obscenity in India, as elsewhere, is the sexualized female body in the visual field, especially the media. Portrayals of women in advertising, sexual displays of female bodies, and cultural depictions of inappropriate clothing in film, TV, and magazines typify (hetero)sexualized excess. Such excess is also represented by suggestive forms of dancing, explicit displays of heterosexual affection in film, TV, videos, cable channels, magazines, public performances involving film celebrities, and so on. Courts constantly adjudicate between popular morality and freedom of expression, sometimes upholding one and sometimes defending the other. Distinctions between obscenity, vulgarity, and indecency are also cited, since freedom of expression is not unmitigated and protecting public morality remains an imperative of governance.

EVEN AS the dialectics of public morality and private liberty appear to drive the juridical and cultural discourses on obscenity in India, they are at best partially relevant. The Introduction to this collection and other essays included herein speak to the limitations of this discursive framework of obscenity. What is curious about the Indian context is the frequent recourse to law in stances taken against obscenity. Charges of obscenity are regularly levied against women performers as well as actors, directors, and artists who depict sexualized female bodies. Representations of non-normative sexualities—for example, Deepa Mehta's film *Fire*, portraying sexual love between two women—are also charged with being obscene. The authority of law is constantly called into effect against film, music videos, public performances, and paintings. Self-defined concerned citizens or political and religious groups register complaints at local police stations and/or file writs in court. Reportedly, thousands of public-interest litigations and criminal complaints on related matters clog up the courts even though few prosecutions actually occur. In most cases, enduring the crisis appears to be worst of it. What is additionally relevant is that charges under obscenity law are typically coupled with other laws, often those militating against religious offenses specified in Chapter XV of the Indian Penal Code. The ire of the Hindu Right against the film *Fire* was fueled by the fact that the two leading women characters' names, Radha and Sita, are among the most revered under canonical Hinduism. Violations of heterosexist respectability and Hinduism are inseparable in this case, and legal charges were filed by the Hindu right under obscenity as well as under religious offenses law.

This chapter takes the recurrent recourse to obscenity law as its starting point in order to reconsider the framework of morality and liberty. The argument develops from three cases. The first case has to do with public wrath and legal charges of obscenity against a beloved icon of Tamil-language film based in Southern India, the second with the Hindu Right's hounding of India's best-known painter, M. F. Husain, and the third pertains to the persecution of non-normative sexualities in the northern city of Lucknow. Each case brings together the cultural and legal discourses of obscenity and the coupling of obscenity law with a variety of other laws on defamation, public mischief, promoting enmity between religious communities, and "sodomy law." Together, these cases not only foreground the fraught female body that is most often at the heart of popular and feminist debates on censorship.[1] They also underscore the relevance of non-normative sexuality and the ways in which religion and ethnicity deeply mark the terrain of obscenity. While their particulars differ, the three cases help redirect attention to the underpinnings of cultural-legal *practices* that stage more than the contestations of morality and liberty. I suggest that these contestations are feints for calculated incitements aimed at redefining the boundaries of the social body. These cases call attention less to the limits of censorship and liberalism and more to the need to revise theoretical frameworks through which we read juridical and cultural discourses of obscenity.

THE FIRST argument driving this chapter is that routine recourse to obscenity law is a means of policing sexuality and the social body. While building on feminist contributions that draw together sexuality and the social body,[2] I urge reconsideration of our operational understandings of the latter. All too often, the social body that obscenity yokes to sexuality is implied as the nation. Indeed, we have been quick to impugn nationalist discourses for sifting the obscene from the properly sexual, and rightly so. The second argument developed in this chapter suggests the need to multiply our notions of the social body as varyingly predicated upon imagined boundaries of region, ethnicity, and religion, as well as nation. This contingency of the social body suggests that the *mechanism* through which discourses of obscenity stage the policing of sexuality and the social needs to be theorized carefully. In other words, this chapter comes to grips with the means through which legal and cultural registers of obscenity fuse normative sexuality and the normalized social body. Drawing upon theories of the biopolitical, this chapter makes the case that social bodies, howsoever defined, are forged through normative sexuality. Therefore, the third argument presented below is that the routine recourse to obscenity law is a node of biopolitical regulation, by which I mean power's infiltration of life, especially through the forging of the collective.

To engage obscenity law in India is to engage English-language juridical and cultural discourses on obscenity. It is a matter of colonial and postcolonial institutions that the rule of law at the national level is in English. However, this hardly exhausts the many and regionally varied understandings of obscenity; for example, *ashlil,* though generally translated as obscene, is used in more complicated ways in the Hindi language press. Furthermore, obscene materials are hardly limited to English-language based representations; Lawrence Cohen writes about the secretive Hindi-language publications produced around the bacchanalian festival of Holi.[3] These points cannot be understated even as we need to be careful not to assume that discourses in Hindi or Tamil languages are aimed at the regional, while English is about the national. The advantage of focusing on English-language national-level legal discourses of obscenity is that they paradoxically highlight the fact that their object is not necessarily the body of the nation.

Nightmare one: The actor

In September 2005, the renowned Tamil film actor Khusboo is bombarded by charges of obscenity and defamation throughout the state of Tamil Nadu, India. The Tamil edition of a leading English-language newsmagazine, *India Today*, had invited Khusboo's commentary on a national survey about changing sexual attitudes. Although more may have been made of the limitations of the sex survey, the rage is aimed unexpectedly at Khusboo, curiously out of proportion to her remarks, especially given her popularity. Khusboo is not ethnically Tamil, but she has been embraced as an icon of Tamil women. The part that ignites the flames reads: "Our society should liberate itself from such ideas that brides should all be virgins at the time of marriage. No educated man will expect his bride to be virgin at the time of marriage. But when indulging in pre-marital sex, the girl should guard herself against pregnancy and sexually transmitted diseases."[4] That Khusboo has no right to speak on behalf of Tamil women and that she has made "derogatory remarks about the chastity of Tamil women" are allegations first made in a publication of the southern Indian media machine, Sun TV. The crisis ensues. The self-appointed Tamil Protection Movement (TPM), with links to Sun TV, fans the protests against Khusboo. The TPM is forged through a political alliance between two groups with divergent caste-orientations and interests, the Dalit Panthers of India (DPI) and the Pattali Makkal Katchi (PMK). The women's wing of the PMK is at the forefront of the attacks against Khushboo. Thol Thirumavalavan, chief of the TPM, summarizes the main point of the protest: "Khushboo made the remarks on pre-marital sex to justify her own life's experience. She had no right to talk of the chastity of Tamil women."[5] She did not; her commentary was general, not directed specifically at Tamil women or men. A 1990s heartthrob, a deified figure with one temple devoted to her, a cinematic icon of Tamil women, is swiftly pilloried as a "North Indian," Hindi-speaking Gujarati Muslim.[6]

Effigies of Khusboo are burned, volunteers of the DPI storm the office of the South India Film Artistes' Association, demanding an apology from the actress.[7] The apology is issued: "Even in films, I never undertook roles that lowered the image of women," she says. "I have the greatest regard for Tamils, especially Tamil women. If my remarks have hurt anybody's feelings, I tender an apology. I am one among you and will always remain with you."[8] But the protests continue. A competing media source, Jaya TV, with which Khusboo is affiliated, reports that many of those who are gathered for the agitations do not know what has been published;[9] Khusboo is pelted with eggs, tomatoes, and slippers while arriving for an appearance before a magistrate.

Complaints of defamation and obscenity are lodged throughout the state. In Tiruchi, Tamil Nadu, for example, four women lawyers charge Khusboo with committing offenses under Section 292, related to obscenity, and under Sections 504 and 505.[10] Section 504 briefly addresses intentional insult with intent to breach peace, while Section 505 is a lengthy discussion of what constitutes public mischief—circulating rumors and reports that are meant to incite mutiny in the military, to incite fear or alarm, to incite harm against another group, or to promote ill will among groups, especially at a place of worship or religious event. In other cases, defamation charges are invoked against Khusboo through Section 499 (representations intended to cause harm to the reputation of a person) and Section 500 (threat of injury to a person, reputation, or property).

If charges of obscenity under Section 292 seem to relate to the substance of what is said, then the charges of public mischief and defamation appear to be about intentionality. Obscenity is predictably derived from women's heterosexuality; mere mention of the possibility that (Tamil) women may be sexually active prior to marriage is enough provocation for self-appointed protectionists of Tamil cultural nationalism. That Khusboo recommends change in social attitudes, particularly men's expectations of women's sexuality, is seen as incitement to depravity, intended to cause public mischief and defame Tamil women. Her position as an insider/outsider throws suspicion on her intentions and makes what she says obscene. Her popularity as a representation of Tamil women accounts for why she is seen as "speaking for"[11] them and maligning Tamil culture, which leads to her being repositioned as a "Hindi-speaking Gujarati Muslim." She is caught between Tamil cultural nationalism's resistance to northern cultural and political hegemony and its anti-Muslim taint. Her position as a Tamil-speaking icon of Tamil women accounts for why her remarks can be easily appropriated as pertaining to Tamil culture, and her non-Tamil status accounts for why the remarks can be presented as an attack; how dare *she* serve as a "proxy and portrait" of Tamil women and culture.[12] The obscenities are seemingly manifold.

The involvement of the key players—the TPM, various contingents of the DPI and the PMK, Sun TV and its competitor, Jaya TV—indicates that charges of obscenity are fraught with more than women's sexualities, and, in this case, are the effects of political expediency and Tamil cultural nationalism. Informed commentaries speak to how these vituperations are the result of several factors:[13] Khusboo led an earlier charge against a film director and member of TPM, who equated actresses with prostitution, and this was considered payback time; Khusboo hosts a popular quiz show on Sun TV's competitor channel, Jaya TV; the Dalit party, composed of those who have been historically refused a place in the Brahmanical caste hierarchy, and the PMK, which represents lower caste interests, have dipped into the well of Tamil nationalism for electoral purposes, a nationalism first whipped up by the upper-caste Dravid Munnetra Kazhagam (DMK) party in the interests of electoral politics by the early 1970s.[14] These complicated political, caste-based, and media-staged battles nonetheless are waged over women's sexual respectability, and Tamil nationalism draws the lines of belonging and battle as necessary.

Nightmare two: The artist

A furor erupts in February 2006 against India's best-known painter and living legend, Maqbool Fida Husain. This is the most recent in a series of Hindu fundamentalist–led uproars, triggered by an abstraction of the Indian map onto a painting of a female figure and a *charkha* (wheel). The body-map is a vibrant, stunning red, offset by a black outline, the blue of the ocean and the darkened silhouette of a male yogi. Reminiscent of the body-map in Mahasweta Devi's stories, made famous in the United States by Gayatri Chakravorty Spivak, that illustrates the violence rendered on the body of tribal women by Indian nationalism and the state, this depiction is also anguished. It invokes the Hindu Right–led and state-supported pogrom against Muslim women and communities in Gujarat in 2002. The names of cities—Benares, Delhi, Gujarat, among others—literalize the female body as map; Chennai-based Apparao Galleries entitles it "Bharatmata" (Mother-India). The painting is sold to a private collector in 2004 and has never been publicly displayed,[15] but that does not prevent as many as sixty-six criminal cases being filed in a number of states and in New Delhi on grounds of obscenity and outraging religious sentiments.[16] An apology by Husain for hurting people's sentiments does not prevent the vandalism of an exhibition later in 2006 in London or the threats of violence—The Hindu Personal Law Board President, Ashok Pandey, announces Rs. 51 crore (Indian Rs. 10 million) to "eliminate" the artist, and, in a show of sympathy, Congress Minority Cell leader Akhtar Baig offers Rs. 11 lakh (Indian Rs. 100,000) to any "patriot" for the painter's hands.[17]

Husain is a complex figure. Over 90 years old, he has been feted with some of the most prestigious honors by Indian governments, including the post of honorary member of the upper house of parliament. He is a prolific painter, self-described as Muslim and secular, born in a place of Hindu pilgrimage in the state of Maharashtra, first employed as a billboard painter, a founding member of the Progressive Artists' Group, public figure, and, as is frequently mentioned, a consummate showman. He is flamboyant, accused of crass commercialism for pandering to the market in which his works are the most expensively valued. He responds, "Even marketing is an art form. I've created a whole new phenomenon of how to market. And I am not defensive about that."[18]

The conditions under which Husain is the most maligned painter of the Hindu right wing are also complex. Husain was first deliberately targeted in 1996 when members of the Bajrang Dal, the youth wing of the organization Vishwa Hindu Parishad (VHP), destroyed Husain's paintings and damaged the gallery in Ahmedabad. The trigger? A 1976 sketch of the Hindu goddess of knowledge and the arts, Saraswati, which was dredged up by Om Nagpal in the right-wing Hindu journal *Vichar Mimansa* as a "nude" desecration.[19] With its greeting-card–like outline of the goddess and her sitar, a lotus in one hand, this simple and bold sketch was part of the preparation for a fully clothed painting of Saraswati made for the O. P. Jindal industrial family.[20] Nagpal's article was the basis upon which the Maharashtra Minister for Culture and leader of the sectarian right-wing Shiv Sena party, Pramod Navalkar, filed criminal charges with Mumbai Police against Husain for promoting enmity between different groups of people on the grounds of religion and acting to insult religious feelings and beliefs.

Then in 1998, Bajrang Dal members stormed into and vandalized Husain's residence in Mumbai, this time on the pretext of a lithograph displayed at an exhibition at the Academy of Art and Literature, New

Delhi, based on the mythic tale of the rescue of Sita by Hanuman.[21] Produced in 1984, this depiction stays true to the epic story in which Sita rides on Hanuman's tail; the point of contention for the Bajrang Dal, however, was Sita's gray, seemingly unclothed figure. Seen in the context of Husain's other work from the time period related to the two Indian/Hindu epics, female and male nude figures are everywhere. The canvases belie a pre-occupation with the epics, archetypes of human quandaries and fallibilities, and the mythic figures that embody them. Female and male figures do not appear to be provocative or eroticized so much as they are illustrations of the battle between good and evil that rages within each person.

Over the last decade, hundreds of complaints have been filed with the police in various parts of the country, there have been dozens of marches and burnings of Husain effigies, and dozens of criminal writs have been submitted in courts in cities such as Mumbai, Delhi, and Bhopal.[22] Indeed, subsequent to the Bharatmata controversy, the Supreme Court responded to Husain's request that the writs from the states of Maharashtra, Gujarat, and Madhya Pradesh be combined and that he should not have to appear in numerous courts and cities.[23] The writs against Husain are based on Sections 292 and 294 of the Indian Penal Code, relating to obscenity, Section 153-A (promoting enmity between different communities based on religion, race, place of birth and language, etc.), Section 295-A (deliberate and malicious act to outrage religious feelings of any class by insulting its religion or religious beliefs), and Section 298 (uttering words with deliberate intent to wound religious feelings of any person).

Since 1996, Husain has been ensnared in a maelstrom of obscenity charges elaborated on the grounds of female sexual representation and religious difference. Who he is and what he paints are collapsed to orchestrate a crisis around the female nude. As art historian Tapati Guha-Thakurta notes, the female nude is a source of deep ambivalence within Indian art history and is precariously situated in the growing rift between representations of high art and popular disapproval, between the aesthetic and the moral, between modern art and the religious, between the erotic and the obscene.[24] The decade-long targeting of Husain, Guha-Thakurta argues, is due to his status as a prominent, venerated artist, embodying the modern, the secular, and the national, coupled with the accident of his religion. Implicit in Guha-Thakurta's analysis, but necessary to underscore, is that the battle is framed by the Hindu right wing as the struggle to protect the sanctity of *Hindu* goddesses and Hinduism. Nagpal asks maliciously, why could Husain not "paint his mother and sister in this modern art style?" "Why does he paint a Hindu goddess in such a disrespectful manner? Why doesn't he paint Allah?"[25] The strategy is simple and insidious—to show that Hinduism is under attack. The brunt of this irony—that the predominant hegemonic Brahmanical form of Hinduism can be under assault—is borne by religious minorities, especially Indian Muslims, who are framed as the "enemy within." Hindu goddesses, not gods, become the specific sites upon which the dirty politics of religion, ethnic cultural nationalism, heterosexuality, and masculinity is violently enacted. Obscenity is cited as sexual and religious violence, and used in turn to inflict violence on others.

Nightmare three: The foot soldiers

On July 7, 2001, police in Lucknow, a city in the state of Uttar Pradesh, raid and seal the offices of Bharosa Trust and Naz Foundation International (NFI), two affiliated non-governmental organizations (NGOs) working on HIV/AIDS-related issues. The program manager of Bharosa Trust, Parmeshwar Nair, is arrested with another of its workers, Mohammad Shahid, after which the police take into custody the Director of NFI, Arif Jafar, and a worker, Sudhees Kumar. The police appropriate educational material and items used for the demonstration of safe sex practices. Within a day, stories reportedly fueled by Lucknow police make headlines in English-language newspapers, about "gay clubs" being run from the two offices, and of pornographic materials and "sex tools" used for nefarious purposes. Senior Superintendent of Police Brij Bhushan Bakshi is quoted in a Hindi language newspaper as saying that all the accused would be sent to jail for polluting Indian culture.[26]

The events leading up to these scurrilous reports are as follows. A man files a First Information Report (FIR) with the police that on July 6, 2001, he was lured by another man, who stopped him along a deserted road and sodomized him. Activists close to the case believe that this report was the result of the complainant not being paid for sex. Based on this report, the police raid the cruising park where the complainant says he was picked up, and arrest more people, including an outreach worker from Bharosa Trust. This worker leads police to the office of Bharosa Trust, and the raids and additional arrests ensue.

Nine people are arrested, four of whom are members of the two NGOs. The police charge them under Sections 377 (unnatural offenses), 292 (obscenity), 120b (criminal conspiracy), and 109 (abetment). Oddly enough, the men are also charged under Section 60 of the Copyright Act and Sections 3 and 4 of the Indecent Representation of Women Act in regard to the educational materials seized from the offices. Applications for bail are rejected twice until they are granted on August 17, and the four men are finally released on August 21, 2001. In their 45 days in prison, the men are beaten, denied food, forced to drink sewer water, and refused treatment when they are ill. The Sessions Judge initially denies bail on the grounds that "they were a group of persons indulging in these activities and are polluting the entire society by encouraging young persons and abetting them for committing the offense of sodomy; that the investigation is still under progress; that the offenses are being committed in an organized manner."[27]

If the extra-legal police activities invoke heterosexist nationalism, then these two scenarios remind us that matters are always more complicated. The curious and troubling aspects of this case in Lucknow are the particular mix of charges—"unnatural sex," obscenity, and criminal conspiracy—not to say anything about charges of copyright violations and indecent representation of women. Section 377, or the "sodomy law," is another legacy of the British colonial state, and though the language is imprecise, it is widely interpreted to criminalize same-sex sexual practices. Section 377 is a cognizable law (arrest without warrant) and non-bailable (bail can be applied for only after arrest), but also one that requires medical proof of unnatural sex. No such substantiation could be established for the four HIV/AIDS workers under arrest. The imprisonment of and violence against the four men in Lucknow was never about allegations of sexual acts or sex practices; as the initial false newspaper reports and the Sessions Judge indicate, they are about the precariousness of heterosexuality. Enforcement or prosecution of Section 377 requires that a complaint be filed, which did not occur in the case of the four men. Rather, they were rounded up in police raids on the NGO offices, where they were seized alongside educational materials and implements. Their violation was seen to lie in circulating representations of sex, in speaking for the unmentionable subject of non-normative sexual practices. But, perhaps, their most egregious transgression was that these men were seen to stand in place of obscenity itself.

On July 10, 2001, within days of the arrests and amidst the media frenzy, the *Times of India*, a leading English-language newspaper, broke the story that the Central Intelligence Bureau had tipped off the Government of India about the spreading of "gay culture" in seven cities, including Lucknow.[28] Reportedly, the intelligence bureau was pressed into service to monitor the flow of funds to NGOs in India, since they were coming from Europe and Canada, with the so-called involvement of Pakistani nationals. The news article suggests that although the intelligence bureau report could not be corroborated, NGOs such as Bharosa Trust and NFI were operating as "gay clubs" and "sex rackets"; thus, the report implies that the NGOs were subtly propagating gay culture through foreign aid.

EACH OF these three cases speaks to the nightmarish links between obscenity and cultural politics within which famous figures and ordinary people are caught. Juridical and cultural discourses on obscenity cohere around representations of sexual excess—wrought through women's (hetero)sexualities, as goddesses are anthropomorphized, and non-normative sexualities, particularly males who have sex with males.[29] What makes these cases stand out from the everyday interplay of obscenity and cultural politics is their intensity, as happenings are manipulated into events, events into crises.

Juridical, cultural, sexual

Obscenity laws were first introduced into late-nineteenth-century colonial India and later incorporated into the post-independence Indian Penal Code. The imperial underpinnings of a juridical system designed to contain the threats of obscenity in Britain and its colonies are addressed by Deanna Heath. Bringing together the analytics of race, nation, and empire, Heath argues that attempts to regulate obscenity were aimed at protecting the superiority of the British "race" and nation from the corrupting influences of the publications and objects originating in the colonies as much as at protecting the colonies from the voluminous exports emanating from Britain.[30] "Purity" crusades were waged in Britain in ways that reverberated in the colonies, especially through the signing of international conventions against the transnational trade in obscene publications and objects. Although the colonial government in India was a reluctant participant in the 1910 International Agreement for the Suppression of Obscene Publications, it was more enthusiastic about the 1923 International Convention for the Suppression of the Circulation of and Traffic in Obscene Publications.[31] According to Heath, Indian colonial officials' earlier reluctance stemming from the belief that India was more "sinned against than sinning" was offset by the need to defend India's civilization from Western vice by regulating obscenity.[32]

If juridical attempts at curtailing obscenity in colonial India emerged from circulations between metropole and colonies, then, as Charu Gupta argues, they were never simply about Victorian perceptions of decency and propriety.[33] In the only book-length treatment of obscenity in colonial India, Gupta notes that emergent concerns with obscenity at the time were equally motivated by the moral concerns of an emergent middle-class and elite Indian nationalism goading British intervention. British and Indian moralists shared anxieties about the transmission of sexually explicit materials, "dirty" literature, and sexual literature couched as scientific or modern.[34] Indeed, for British officials in India the task was doubly challenging—to protect against Western importations of obscenity but also its indigenous versions. It is within the context of British Orientalism and the "woman question" at the center of colonial and anti-colonial encounters that obscenity came to hinge on the control of female sexuality and the restriction of sex to procreation, not pleasure.[35]

Identifying a second strand as "politically obscene," Gupta notes that these materials blended sexuality, politics, and emergent religious divides.[36] Since the mid-nineteenth century, Hindu writers in Uttar Pradesh, a state in northern India, had slandered Islam and its prophet and had deliberately linked the alleged debauchery of past Muslim rulers to the breakdown of the state and public order. Few Muslim rulers were spared charges of lechery or dissolution, and, by the 1920s, these claims had expanded to allegations of rape and forcible marriage of Hindu women by Muslim men, claims that echo even today. Indeed, Cohen's description of secretive literature, mentioned earlier, produced during Holi in the city of Benares, also in the state of Uttar Pradesh, points to similar fantasies. Cohen describes these publications, locally marked as obscenity, as not only including men sexually penetrating other men, unequal sexual exchanges among men through traffic in women, and critiques of the state, but also the rape Hindu men must perform on Muslim women in order to justify and counter their own sexual fantasies about the threat posed by Muslim men to Hindu women![37]

Rather than "political obscenity," Sections 292–294 of the IPC broadly target the intersections of sexuality and representation in ways that require judicial interpretation. Section 292 specifically prohibits the circulation, selling, printing, advertising, hiring, and profiting from obscene representations in the form of books, writings, paintings, and the like. Section 292A extends the same prohibitions to materials intended for purposes of blackmail. Any person who benefits from or aids in making available obscene materials to persons below the age of 20 is liable under Section 293. These juridical provisions are the result of legal amendments over the years that have attempted to clarify the meaning and scope of the provisions, with the most thoroughgoing revisions dating to 1969. Intended to introduce contemporary standards into archaic laws, Vishnu D. Sharma and F. Wooldridge note that the 1969 amendments were heavily influenced by the 1959 Obscene Publications Act in England.[38]

In their overview of Indian obscenity law, Sharma and Wooldridge observe that, since the 1925 version of Section 292 lacked a definition of obscenity, the courts used the *Hicklin* test, and the only available exception to obscenity was provided on religious grounds.[39] In contrast, the 1969 amendments continued to militate against the circulation and sale of obscene literature, while ensuring that materials justifiably for public good or with a bona fide religious purpose were exempt. Exceptions were expanded to include "public good," interests of science, literature, religious purposes, a public servant discharging his functions, as well as representations that are protected under the Ancient Monuments and Archaeological Sites and Remains Act of 1958. Most importantly, a definition of obscenity is given which remains in effect today: "(that which) is lascivious or appeals to prurient interest or if its effect or (where it comprises two or more distinct items) the effect of one of its items, if taken as a whole, is such as to tend to deprave and corrupt persons who are likely, having regard to all relevant circumstances, to read, see or hear the matter contained or embodied in it." Notwithstanding the brief mention of obscene acts in public in Section 294, the laws anticipate and seek to manage sexual transgressions in the realm of representation. The laws not only seek to draw lines between the obscene and the erotic, the moral and the indecent, but also come to be routinely pinned on sexual transgressions involving female heterosexuality and deviant sexualities.[40] The "politically obscene" described by Gupta appears to be accommodated under Sections 292–294, insofar as it may be lascivious, but more likely under the sections on defamation (499–500), if it appears to be non-sexual in nature.

Despite these attempts to revise and refine obscenity law in India, the meaning of obscenity remains vague and ill defined. Judges play a key role in interpreting the law and negotiating prurience and public good, frequently relying on the Miller test.[41] The persistent impreciseness of the meaning of obscenity is thought to contribute to abuse of the law through routine and frivolous legal filings. Especially since it is years before judicial decisions are announced, filing legal charges promises to tie defendants in court for a protracted period of time. One response is to call for further clarity in order both to prevent such abuse and to encourage successful prosecutions. However, in a land-mark decision in December 2006, the Indian Supreme Court ruled against a public-interest litigation asking to curb explicit photographs and ads published in newspapers, on the grounds that a blanket defini-tion of obscenity would hurt freedom of the press.

While the outcome of court charges may be long in arriving, announcements of legal charges of obscenity quickly garner media and public attention. The authority of law is used to leverage the media, and the outcome is a very public drawing and redrawing not only of what counts as obscenity but also of what counts as respectability. On the one hand, Khusboo's remarks are crammed into the codification of obscenity under Section 292—that by posing the very possibility of women's pre-marital sexual activity, the words can corrupt or cause depravity. On the other hand, and this seems to me more important, what is not debated is whether women's pre-marital sexual desire is nor-mal or natural; rather, it appears that Khusboo's deeper offense lies in publicly suggesting that women are sexually active prior to marriage. Unlike sexual normality, which is tied to the individual, sexual respect-ability is essentially a social criterion through which individuals and groups are tied to the collective. That the charges of "unnatural sex" (Section 377) need to be trumped up in the case of the four workers in Lucknow while the police release false reports of "gay clubs" and "sex rackets" further confirms that the sexual is seen essentially as a matter of the social.

Alongside and through the incitement of cultural and legal dis-courses on sexual respectability is also an incitement of discourses of the social body. Sexual excess and its correlates of depravity, lascivious-ness, and indecency, to name a few, are reinforced as intrinsically con-tagious, as easily corrupting the social body. In Khusboo's case, it would have been possible simply to ignore the comments or refute her opin-ions publicly without heaping scorn on her. But the hue and cry serves to reconstitute the Tamil community as essentially fragile and easily undermined. Not surprisingly, then, Khusboo's words on the social acceptance of pre-marital female sexuality are seen as a direct assault on the Tamil community, even though her remarks are aimed at women in general. In the other two cases as well, protecting the collective— whether of Hindus or Indians—requires constant vigilance and a virile masculinity. In Husain's case, not only are his visual representations deliberately provoked by the Hindu Right as the sexualization of Hindu goddesses, but they are actively presented as attacks on the integrity of the so-called community of Hindus. The conjoined use of obscenity and sodomy law in the Lucknow case further speaks to the threat that sexual excess poses to the social body, this time seen as the nation.

By excoriating Khusboo as not-Tamil, the internal and external frontiers of the collective become the same. Those at the internal frontiers of the body—by virtue of religion, ethnicity, same-sex sexualities, or gender, caste, and class—are also markers of its external frontiers. It is not so much that the external boundaries of the collective are being defined as that the external and internal boundaries are being collapsed into one another purportedly in the interests of the collective. That in each of the cases obscenity law is coupled with a constellation of other legal charges attests to anxieties regarding the expansive injuries caused by sexual excess. Defamation, breach of peace, and intent to hurt religious feelings, among others, are the laws that signal concerns about protecting the so-called integrity of the social body.

If national-level laws and policies of law enforcement stabilize the appearance of a singular social body, then regional, cultural, and political differences interact with their interpretations and enactments. In 2004, the Delhi High Court ruled on eight cases against Husain related to his sketch of Saraswati, a sketch of another mythic figure, Draupadi, and paintings of the well-known Hindi film actress Madhuri Dixit. This was in the wake of the first politicization of Husain's work in 1996. The offenses included obscenity, indecent representations of women, promoting enmity between religious groups, and deliberately outraging the religious feelings of a group. The Supreme Court had ruled that the various cases filed in the states of Bihar, Madhya Pradesh, and elsewhere be bundled together under the purview of the High Court of Delhi. Delhi High Court Justice Kapoor dismissed the cases against Husain, but only on a technicality. At odds with the defense arguments that the artwork was done without any malicious intentions, the judge nonetheless dismissed the eight charges on the grounds that the charges had to be filed with the cognizance of the central or state government. Even as the authority of a centralized legal system prevailed, the justice severely chastised Husain for hurting Hindu sentiments. He wrote, "Under the garb of freedom of expression no person can be allowed to hurt the religious feelings of any class of people. This should be known more to the petitioner who belongs to a different religion" (Crl. M(M) 420/2001). Husain's legal victory was no vindication, as the judge deployed the centralized legal structure to protect the integrity of a specific and hegemonic social body, namely, Hindus.

A singular notion of the social body is not at work here. Rather, it varies across each of these cases—Tamil nationalism; Hindutva, which invokes Hindus as a community distinct from non-Hindus, especially Christians and Muslims; and (putatively secular-but-Hindu) Indian nationalism. Notwithstanding the provision that the Indian penal code does not extend to the northernmost and embattled states of Jammu and Kashmir, obscenity law and other citations from the penal code operate at the national level. Yet the notion of the collective at stake is neither always national nor uniform. Further, these forms of imagined collectives are not concentric circles expanding from the regional to the national. They are more accurately represented as Venn Diagrams of overlap and difference; for example, Tamil nationalism frequently goes against the grain of what is seen as north-dominated Indian nationalism. It is to theorizing the ways in which discourses of obscenity illuminate the mechanism that ties the sexual to varying notions of the social body that I now turn.

Sexuality, social bodies, and biopolitics

The focus on obscenity across these three cases draws attention to the fact that sexuality is at the heart of how social bodies are fabricated. Sexuality helps forge, produce, and stabilize the collective. Sexuality is not merely a fault line of the collective, sifting normality and its other. Rather, sexuality is essential to how social collectives are imagined, which explains the pre-occupations with it. The three cases indicate that at stake are not matters of individual bodies or sexualities, even though the brunt of the assaults was borne by specific individuals. Rather, the crises proceed through the domain of sexuality to the integrity and continuity of the collective body. Precisely because sexuality is foundational to the production of the collective, it is saturated with anxieties of normality, respectability, depravity, irregularities, and more. Concerns related to obscenity articulate these anxieties and become an available placeholder. Representations of sexualities, particularly female or deviant, that are considered obscene may be politically motivated, but they also echo underlying anxieties about the fabrication and continuity of the community, howsoever defined.

The broad use of obscenity speaks to how sexuality both constitutes and endangers social bodies. In the Lucknow witch-hunt, the putative threat to the collective makes sense only if we concede that same-sex sexuality may undermine heteronormativity. The possibility of "gay clubs" and "sex rackets," of consensual same-sex practices and sex work, fans anxieties about reproductive and non-reproductive heteronormativity precisely because of its brittleness, precisely because heteronormativity is seen as the lifeline of the community, and precisely because any threat to heteronormativity constitutes a threat to the political community. At issue are not only same-sex sexualities but anything that may be perceived as a threat to heteronormativity and its rightful place in marriage and community. Interpretations of Khusboo's words strike as blows to the cultural and biological survival of the collective. Anything other than respectable sexuality calls into question for her critics not only the morality of Tamil women but also heterosexual marriage, inheritance, class, and caste lines, and normative masculinity.

Foucault's concept of biopolitics, as the fabrication and regulation of the human collective into a "population," gets closest to theorizing the significance of sexuality in the production of the social body. Biopolitics, for Foucault, entails defining, assessing, managing, and policing the notion of population and reveals the need to regulate it on behalf of collective interests. Births, reproduction, deaths, disease, health, life expectancy, and more make up that morass of conditions through which populations are forged. Biopolitics alerts us to the kind of violence necessary to forge such wholeness.

Central to biopolitics is Foucault's premise that regulation proceeds by infiltrating life, not through the threat of death. It is motivated toward regularization, not disciplining. Clarifying what he first laid out in the last section of the *History of Sexuality, Volume 1,* Foucault suggests succinctly in his lecture at the College de France on March 17, 1976: "it is, in a word, a matter of taking control of life and the biological processes of man-as-species and of ensuring that they are not disciplined, but regularized."[42] A few sentences later, he elaborates on the biopolitical technology that is focused on managing life, unlike the pre-occupation with death of an earlier modality of power, namely, sovereignty: "It is continuous, scientific, and it is the power to make live. Sovereignty took life and let live. And now we have the emergence of a power that I would call the power of regularization and it, in contrast, consists in making live and letting die."[43]

For Foucault, this presents a new relationship between life and history because even though life is posed as biological it is, in fact, penetrated by history's techniques of knowledge and power.[44] It also presents the growing importance of the norm over the threat of law. The kinds of phenomena that biopolitics is concerned with, Foucault insists, are aleatory—unpredictable, uncertain—and must be studied within the population over a period of time. Through the technologies directed at improving the life and quality of the population, controlling the random and the accidental through calculation and forecast, biopolitical regulation is aimed at controlling mortality, not wielding the threat of death.

The nexus between life and populations suggested by Foucault has spurred scholarship along two dimensions—the terrain of biology, medicine, and science within which questions of health, genetics, and disease are framed;[45] and the forging of political communities by defining their exceptions, whether through the status of refugee, terrorist, or through the fault lines of race.[46] The concept of the biopolitical is useful in these disparate dimensions precisely because it turns attention to the deeper questions of life and the making of the collective. The concept underscores the various arenas through which "populations" are continually fashioned—for example, at the national level this fashioning occurs through census surveys, by assessing demographics, and through disease and health indicators, among others.

The preoccupations with obscenity in the context of India, especially in the three cases described here, underscore the significance of sexuality to the forging of the collective, to the nexus between life and politics. It is curious that even though Foucault first elaborates the concept of the biopolitical in *History of Sexuality, Vol. 1,* sexuality has so easily fallen out of our theorizing of it. In *Homo Sacer,* Giorgio Agamben's thinking on the biopolitical lays bare the politicization of life through which (Western) political community is wrought. Focusing on the (deracialized, degendered, desexualized) stock figure of the refugee or the idiom of the camp, Agamben seeks to expose ways in which the state of exception that drives a wedge between natural rights and the rights of citizenship comes to be a foundational, lasting characteristic of political community. In so doing, Agamben significantly revises Foucault's attempts at linking disciplinary power that operates at the level of the body and biopolitical power at the level of the collective, and yet what is elided is Foucault's necessary insight: sexuality is the mechanism that links individuals to the collective and connects disciplinary power to the biopolitical.[47]

Similarly, Achille Mbembe offers a thought-provoking revision of Foucault's reflections on the biopolitical through the concept of necropolitics, to argue that contemporary life is subjugated to the power of death. Using historical and contemporary examples, drawn from Nazi death camps, slave plantations, the occupation of Palestine, as well as sustained violence and genocide in Africa, Mbembe, like Agamben, neglects a reading of power and sovereignty deepened by attention to the ways in which the domain of sexuality serves as a pathway of power; for example, HIV/AIDS is significantly absent as a crucible of the bio-political and the necro-political in Mbembe's analysis.

Rather than auxiliary, sexuality is directly instrumental to the biopolitical forging of collectives. This approach helps us reconsider how life, disease, genocide, demographics—the numerous indices of population, in fact—are grounded in the domain of sexuality, especially heteronormativity. Despite the various complexities of political expediency, the three cases can assume the proportions that they do precisely because the significance of sexuality, articulated through obscenity, strikes at the heart of the collective, its continuity, its stabilization. For the same reason, it is important for some publics to chisel away at representations of indecency or lasciviousness through public protests, the police, and the authority and sanctity of legal provisions. Drawn out discussions in multiple public realms are far more effective than quick, successful convictions from this vantage point.

The three cases also say something more about the functioning of the biopolitical. Precisely in their shape as events, as crises, they do not work in the same way as census surveys and population growth indices. In contrast to the regularization and standardization techniques of bio-politics, these events appear to be irregularities. Yet the irregularities happen with enough regularity, as it were, to make us rethink the conjunctions between regularity and irregularities, between standardization and crises, between making predictable the random and relying on its unpredictabilities. Seen this way, the nodes of biopolitical strategy are not just institutions of governance that shape demographic and population discourses. Rather, the nodes of the biopolitical span structures of governance, institutions such as the media, as well as political groups, parties, and individuals.

Furthermore, while the connotation of the social body has specific meanings within a Western liberal tradition, the social body that is forged through the anxieties and incitements of obscenity in the Indian context needs to be appreciated as not just the national, but also the transnational, the regional, the intra-national ethnic regional, and the transnational religious, among others. Biopolitics is not merely the regulation of social bodies as nation or the political community as the nation-state. Rather, it is the mechanism through which power forges and fuses heteronormative sexuality and the hegemonic social body.

The predictability of charges of obscenity, recourse to obscenity laws, especially with few indications of successful prosecution, needs to be rethought as the forging of hetero-collectives through the use of bio-political strategies. Considering the significance of sexuality to the collective draws connections between the various nodes of the biopolitical, including pre-occupations with obscenity, census surveys, demographics, immigration policies, the national body, sovereignty, and regional cultural nationalism. Cutting sharply across these various terrains, not in any monolithic or predictable way, is the domain of sexuality. Seen thus, the three cases described here make us take seriously how Khusboo's utterances, Husain's paintings, and the four NGO members' work could cause such anxieties, how these crises could be tactically effective in fueling such anxieties, and how matters of obscenity are directly instrumental to these anxieties. These three cases are imperatives not to underrate the obsession with obscenity and, through it, sexuality's foundational role in the shaping of social bodies.

Concluding remarks

The perceived need to protect the integrity of social bodies explains the preoccupations with obscenity law in the Indian context. The discourses of obscenity serve to expand but also to protectively retract and retrench the contours of social bodies. Obscenity and its correlates—indecency, lasciviousness, moral turpitude—are seen to corrupt the core fabric of social bodies in ways that warrant attention equal to political instability, war, poverty, and hunger. Obscenity law in India offers a commentary on the foundational significance of sexuality to public order and the threat of unregulated sexuality to individuals and social bodies. The cultural and legal discourses of obscenity demand that we acknowledge sexuality's foundational significance, especially reproductive and non-reproductive heteronormativity, to the forging of collectives. Obscenity is as much a synecdoche of sexuality as it is of the collective, and while we are likely to concede easily the multiplicity of sexualities, it is necessary to press the issue that there isn't a singular notion of the collective and that notions of the collective are contingent. The point is not merely to insist on the plural over the singular. The point, instead, is to grapple with the ways in which discourses of obscenity activate social bodies understood not only as national but also as factors in religious, ethnic, and cultural identity.

Turning to the biopolitical alerts us to the underlying mechanism through which sexuality serves the regulation of social bodies. Sexuality is the chain link between life and political collectives, between life and power. The unrelenting preoccupations with obscenity and sexual excess bear testimony to sexuality not as ancillary but as central to social bodies and to the imagination of political community. These legal/cultural incitements are the means through which power fuses and reinforces heteronormative sexuality and hegemonic social bodies.

On May 8, 2008, Delhi High Court Justice Sanjay Kishan Kaul (CRL Revision Petition No. 114/2007) dismissed the cases against M.F. Husain.[48] In a decision hailed by liberal-leaning public intellectuals, artists, and supporters of Husain, Justice Kaul sorted through the familiar and fraught terrain of public morality and artistic liberty. Opening his lengthy statement by paraphrasing Pablo Picasso—that where art is chaste, it is no longer art—Justice Kaul went on to juxtapose obscenity law in India with that in the U.S., Canada, and Australia. The outcome was an undoubtedly liberal legal endorsement of the need to take a work in its entirety, to sort through the distinctions between obscenity, vulgarity, indecency, and pornography, to confirm that sexuality is not synonymous with obscenity, to protect artistic expression while cautioning against Indian puritanical ignorance that is leading to the desecration of art and the abuse of law. The Justice's statement can be set up as a tussle between the right to artistic liberty and the requirements of public morality, between the right of expression and the effect of transgression. That this decision and statement uphold the right of expression and artistic liberty is exactly what resounds in the numerous endorsements by public intellectuals.

Yet, to merely read Justice Kaul's statement in this way omits and elides the imperatives of biopolitical governance and the production and regulation of the social body. In Justice Kaul's statement, the tug between public morality and artistic liberty is mitigated by the notion of social stability. Unlike the United States, he noted, India has no absolute right to freedom of speech, and while it is up to the state to ensure that it does not impose unreasonable restrictions, the state can introduce restrictions in the interests of the larger social good. Indeed, as Justice Kaul said, there is an inseparable connection between freedom of speech and the stability of society, and the yardstick for determining whether a work is transgressive and offensive is whether it violates the integrity of the social body as whole. The statement upholds the liberty of Husain by paying close attention to the exigencies of sexuality and the social body. For this, Justice Kaul made two primary arguments: he conceded the need to protect the social body by emphasizing that the painting, Bharatmata, is not about the depiction of lust; and, in a more spirited vein, he suggested that Hindus cannot claim to be wounded by the painting for the nation does not only belong to them. Toward the end of the statement, Justice Kaul cautioned against frivolous lawsuits and enjoined the courts not to entertain such abuse. Insofar as the outcome of such writs is incidental to the use of cultural-legal practices to draw and redraw the contours of the social body and its fault lines through the realm of sexuality, such cautions will be unheeded and such entreaties unenforceable.

Notes

1. See, for example, Brinda Bose, ed., *Gender & Censorship* (New Delhi: Women Unlimited, 2006).

2. Carolyn Dean, *The Frail Social Body: Pornography, Homosexuality, and Other Fantasies in Inter-War France* (Berkeley: University of California Press, 2000); Charu Gupta, *Sexuality, Obscenity, Community: Women, Muslims, and the Hindu Public in Colonial India* (New Delhi: Permanent Black, 2001); Lynda Nead, *Female Desire: Art, Obscenity and Sexuality* (London and New York: Routledge, 1992).

3. Lawrence Cohen, "Holi in Banaras and the *Mahaland* of Modernity," *GLQ: A Journal of Lesbian and Gay Studies* 2 (1995): 399-424, at 399.

4. Tushar Dhara, "The Khushboo Case File: Reverse Culture Jamming," *Sarai Reader 2006: Turbulence* (New Delhi: Sarai Media Lab, 2006), 388–400.

5. Arvind Narrain, http://www.boloji.com/wfs5/wfs515.htm, consulted on January 27, 2007.

6. Gujarat is a state in Western India. By maligning Khusboo as Hindi-speaking, Gujarati, and Muslim, she is being interpellated as an outsider and as anti-Tamil.

7. "Khushboo's Comments Stir Controversy," http://in.rediff.com/movies/2005/sep/26khushboo.htm, consulted on January 27, 2007.

8. Ibid.

9. Vaasanthi, "Spectacle of Bigotry," *India Today*, December 5, 2005: 58.

10. http://www.tribuneindia.com/2005/20050928/nation.htm#17, consulted on January 27, 2007.

11. I refer, of course, to the important distinctions between representation in the political sense as "speaking for" and re-presentation in the sense of art or acting, first delineated by Gayatri Chakravorty Spivak. In her influential essay, "Can the Subaltern Speak?," in *Marxism and the Interpretation of Culture*, ed. Cary Nelson and Lawrence Grossberg (Urbana and Chicago: University of Chicago Press, 1988), 271–313, Spivak brilliantly delineates the difference between representation as "speaking for" (*vertreten*) and representation as "re-presentation" (*darstellen*) as in art (275). Spivak's purpose is to call attention to the mechanics of power and complicity at work in Western discourse and its representations of subaltern subjects, and to confound the possibility of a subaltern "voice" that is sought to be recovered. The interplay of discourse, representation, and the subaltern is muddied when examined from the vantage point of these three cases in which the maligned figures are neither quite subaltern, nor quite elite, but simultaneously both. The semiotics and ideologies of representation are expanded to include ire not only at

"speaking for," and "re-presentation" of, Tamil or Hindu icons, but also at the "spoken"— the agent who is emblematic of a broader affiliation, a threat, an obscenity.

12. Ibid, p. 276.

13. The following commentaries are especially useful in contextualizing the furor: S. Anandhi, "Sex and Sensibility in Tamil Politics," *Economic and Political Weekly* 40.47 (November 19, 2005): 4876–77; Dhara, "The Khushboo Case File."

14. Dhara, "The Khushboo Case File," 390.

15. http://www.indianexpress.com/story/11208.html, consulted on February 1, 2007.

16. Suhel Seth, "Has Anyone Seen M. F. Husain?," *Asian Age,* August 21, 2006.

17. http://www.tribuneindia.com/2007/20070121/spectrum/main1.htm, consulted on February 1, 2007.

18. Ibid., consulted on February 2, 2007.

19. http://www.hinduonnet.com/fline/fl1511/15110990.htm, consulted on February 1, 2007. As noted in the article, this unearthing occurred within attempts by the Hindu right wing to "Hinduize" Adivasi (tribal) communities, and efforts to appropriate a religious space around the city of Indore, state of Madhya Pradesh, close to where Husain trained in art.

20. Ibid.

21. Ibid.

22. http://www.hindu.com/thehindu/holnus/484200607250314.htm, consulted on February 2, 2007.

23. http://www.hindu.com/thehindu/holnus/001200607251841.htm, consulted on February 2, 2007.

24. Tapati Guha-Thakurta, *Monuments, Objects, Histories: Institutions of Art in Colonial and Postcolonial India* (New York: Columbia University Press, 2004), 245–53.

25. Ibid.

26. http://www.hinduonnet.com/fline/fl1818/18181130.htm, consulted on February 4, 2007.

27. Ibid.

28. "Gay Culture Started in UP in '98 Itself," July 10, 2001, http://0-web.lexis-nexis.com.library.simmons.edu/universe/document?_m=3e37803139952c0730999a2231199 62f&_docnum=24&wchp=dGLbVzz-zSkVb&_md5=6e8a4425ac5e20ce8a04b49083d5c62f, consulted on February 4, 2007.

29. While the descriptor of males who have sex with males is a contested one, especially in relation to South Asia, I use it here because they are the targeted clients of Bharosa Trust and NFI.

30. Deanna Heath, "Purity, Obscenity and the Making of an Imperial Censorship System," in *Media and the British Empire,* ed. Chandrika Kaul (New York: Palgrave Macmillan, 2006), 160–63.

31. Ibid., 164–66.

32. Ibid., 166.

33. Gupta, *Sexuality, Obscenity, Community,* 32.

34. Ibid., 53.

35. Ibid., 34–37.

36. Ibid., 243.

37. Cohen, "Holi in Banaras," 410–14.

38. Vishnu D. Sharma and F. Wooldridge, "The Law Relating to Obscene Publications in India," *International and Comparative Law Quarterly* 22 (Oct 1973): 632-647, at 636.

39. Ibid., 634–35.

40. Some of the most widely publicized cases historically tried under obscenity appear

to be about deviant sexualities. For example, see Charu Gupta's discussion on the story "Chaklet" (in *Sexuality, Obscenity, Community*), and the numerous feminist writings on renowned writer Ismat Chugtai's widely reprinted story "Lihaaf." It is available online at: http://www.manushi-india.org/pdfs_issues/PDF%20file%20110/9.%20Short%20Story% 20-%20Lihaaf%20%5BThe%20Quilt%5D.pdf or http://connectmedia.waag.org/media. opencultures.net/queer/data/indian/Lihaaf_or_The_Quilt.htm. Also see Jisna Menon's discussion on Sadat Hasan Manto's "Kali Salwaar," in "Unimaginable Fine Communities: Identities in Traffic in Rukhsana Ahmad's *Black Salwar*," *Modern Drama* 48.2 (Summer 2005): 407–27.

41. The Miller test is the benchmark in judicial decisions in Indian courts to determine whether representations fall under the rubric of obscenity. It directly influences judicial interpretations of obscenity law in Indian courts. The Miller test is the result of the 1973 case, *Miller v. California*, 413 U.S. 15. It includes three considerations—whether an average person, applying contemporary community standards, would find that the work, taken as a whole, appeals to the prurient interest; whether the work depicts/describes, in a patently offensive way, sexual conduct or excretory functions; whether the work, taken as a whole, lacks serious literary, artistic, political, or scientific value.

42. Michel Foucault, *"Society Must Be Defended" Lectures at the Collège De France 1975-1976*, trans. David Macey (New York: Picador, 2003), 246–47.

43. Ibid., 247.

44. Ibid., 143.

45. Steven Epstein, *Inclusion: The Politics of Difference in Medical Research* (Chicago: University of Chicago Press, 2007); Aihwa Ong, "Making the Biopolitical Subject: Cambodian Immigrants, Refugee Medicine, and Cultural Citizenship in California," *Social Science and Medicine* 40.9 (1995) 1243-1257;

46. Giorgio Agamben, *Homo Sacer: Sovereign Power and Bare Life* (Palo Alto, CA: Stanford University Press, 1998); Henry Giroux, *Stormy Weather: Katrina and the Politics of Disposability* (Boulder and London: Paradigm Publishers, 2006); Achille Mbembe, "Necropolitics," trans. Libby Meintjes, *Public Culture* 15.1 (2003): 11–40; Jasbir Puar, *Terrorist Assemblages: Homonationalism in Queer Times* (Durham, NC, and London: Duke University Press, 2007).

47. Michel Foucault, *History of Sexuality, Vol. 1: An Introduction*, trans. Robert Hurley (New York: Vintage Books, 1978, 1990), 140.

48. http://lobis.nic.in/dhc/, consulted on April 9, 2009.

"I'm Offended"

The question of offense and especially aesthetic offense has haunted my work for a long time; in fact it might be the subtext of everything I've written. What I mean is this. It's been my experience that in writing a book you start out trying to answer one question and end up unable to answer another question, which then of course comes to seem like the *real* question, generally a far larger one than the more manageable question you started with (which invariably seems trite by the time the book is finished, if it ever actually is). Research projects are impelled into being by both manifest and latent desires: the manifest desire fast loses its mystery, while the latent desire taunts your intelligence and/or self-knowledge, which is one of the reasons it's so difficult to reread one's published work, which always seems somehow deficient by the time it hits print. One of the ironies of my own career is being someone with a book about pornography on her vitae—a book generally regarded as more in favor of than opposed to pornography (though personally I'd hesitate to classify it as "pro-porn")—though one whose author remains rather offended by the subject matter whose offensiveness she meant to explicate and thus defang. No doubt one of the things that motivated me to write that book in the first place was wanting to understand why I found pornography offensive at a visceral level while simultaneously feeling vast intellectual and political antipathy toward anyone else with the same response. It remains an unanswered question, though let me add that I've found little in either anti-porn or pro-porn writings that helps illuminate things. Anti-porn theorists tend to be offended at porn because they conflate fantasy with actual violence against women, which I don't find convincing; pro-porn theorists tend to dismiss offense as simply bourgeois and retrograde—and might I add that much of the recent work in the pro-porn vein strikes me as actually more about fandom than explication, determinedly hip in a way that always sets my teeth a little on edge?

So even after hashing over these conflicts in the aforementioned book, big questions gnaw at me still. Not so much *why* pornography is offensive: the answer here is that it's pornography's job to be offensive, systematically locating social boundaries, and then systematically transgressing them. This can be profoundly pleasurable, at least for some, or so I hear. The question that's left over has more to do with the subjectivity of offendability, or the phenomenology of offensiveness: what does it *mean* to be offended, and more to the point, why is this so frequently experienced as unpleasant, even threatening? Why is feeling offended so often connected to anger, as opposed to any of the other available emotions in the human repertoire? Why anger, rather than, say, sadness or confusion?

The lack of attention to such questions in porn studies isn't entirely surprising, especially when you consider how little has been written on what might be termed "negative aesthetics" generally. Take the issue of ugliness, which is not unrelated to aesthetic offense. The history of aesthetics is comprised of volumes upon volumes on the meaning of beauty, with virtually nothing on the ugly. One reason is that aestheticians aren't very sure what it is or what characterizes it. Do things classed as ugly share certain properties? Is ugliness a property of the object itself or does it inhere in the response of the perceiving subject? Being offended seems even more difficult to pin down, despite the percentage of our everyday lives spent in service of offense-avoidance, when you think about it: everything from table manners, to where you can have sex, to disposing of bodily waste, and thousands of other daily rituals. Defy or forget these proprieties and you risk social punishment or ostracization. In fact, it's no exaggeration to say that avoiding the sensation of offense is the central cultural and aesthetic mission of social life as we know it, embodied yet easily offendable creatures that we are.

In the civic realm, the offense-avoidance imperative yields additionally murky and troublesome categories, namely, "obscenity," the rubric under which potentially offended citizens find temporary solace in regulatory maneuvers: pornography zoning, movie ratings, decisions around arts funding, and so on. When the offense-avoidance imperative is pitted against the founding principles of our nation such as freedom of expression, offense-avoidance stands a very good chance of winning, regarded as such an unquestionable right that other rights and freedoms can easily be abridged in its service. The exception is when the offense in question can be shown to have some specifiable social purpose: if the offense can double as a "good citizen" beneath its rough exterior, it may stand a fighting chance. Offense in the name of parody has been declared a form of protected speech by no less a body than the Supreme Court, though other forms of aesthetic offense don't always fare as well. Additionally, offense-curtailment is the goal behind all sorts of new regulations of daily life, namely, the wave of campus and workplace speech codes of the last few of decades.

Still, offense remains a daily problem, and all the codes in the world can't contain the threat. Potential hazards are everywhere, and increasing daily, since the more regulations are instituted, the lower the thresholds of offendability seem to drop. Consider a recent letter in the business section of the *Sunday New York Times*, addressed to a weekly job advice column called "The Career Couch." Queries an anonymous complainant: "You often see two colleagues flirting with each other in the office, and their behavior offends you. What can you do?"[1] The answer, according to the *Times:* speak up, complain to the colleagues, and if that doesn't work, go to the boss. Exactly *why* these flirtatious colleagues are offensive is never in question: offense is its own justification. It's hardly news that the ability to avoid causing offense is linked to receiving a regular paycheck; this has been true from day one of wage slavery, but where will it stop? Those of us laboring in the dingy halls of academia have long habituated ourselves to the fine points of offense-avoidance, having been issued regular directives for years warning the more propriety-challenged in our ranks against creating an "offensive environment" by, for instance, telling jokes in class, despite the fact that the offense-potential of jokes is a continually shifting and capricious category, further complicated by variables like class and gender, not to mention variations in individual toleration levels on the part of joke-recipients. My point is this: even though dramas of offendability are played out minute-by-minute throughout the social world, the etiology and psychology of offense are barely if ever discussed. Instead, the response to the potential of offense is invariably new forms of prohibition and censorship, no doubt because these are easier to institute than it is to attempt to plumb the psychodynamics of offense.

There are, it must be said, different varieties of censorship, and different censoring agencies. As we know, Freud's invention of psychoanalysis was founded on the discovery that certain contents and ideas were prohibited access to consciousness: some censoring agency stood in the way. In Freud's account, however, this is an unconscious process, whose operations aren't immediately available to conscious description. Thus psychical censorship isn't precisely contiguous with social censorship, which is a process undertaken consciously: a social censor knows that he or she intends to enact censorship and can produce a rationale, however unreliable outside observers may take these rationales to be. But before censorship takes a social form, it necessarily takes an interior form. Not psychical censorship, but the intrapsychic experience of *being offended,* by which I mean a *felt* response to some sort of content—generally of a sexual, violent, gross, or sacrilegious nature—that registers on a perceiving subject in particularly marked ways: unpleasantly, possibly viscerally. Being offended is a peculiarly liminal state, I'm suggesting, neither entirely conscious nor entirely unconscious, and additionally liminal in that it's perched uncomfortably in between the psyche and the social. Perhaps this liminality contributes to the difficulty in specifying why it is that being offended is so, well . . . offensive. It also suggests that a phenomenology of offense really has to be the starting point in any social theory of censorship.

WHAT FOLLOWS is a roundabout stab at such an account, by way of an admittedly unlikely case study: the 1994 feature documentary *Crumb,* Terry Zwigoff's biopic about the notoriously vulgar countercultural cartoonist Robert Crumb. Why this film? Mostly because I found my own aesthetic response to it difficult to account for: something unsettled and appalled me about this film, though also fascinated me. Perhaps a more straightforward reason is that the film is itself, self-consciously, a case study on aesthetic offense, pitting Robert Crumb's cartoons against his feminist critics; the critics (to the film's credit), rather than being dismissed or mocked, are offered the opportunity to testify about their various levels of distress at Crumb's pictorial transgressions. For them, Crumb's unrestrained id is an antagonist: they're offended by his blatant sexually aggressive imagery, which they see as propaganda for aggression toward women. Writer Deidre English (interviewed in the film) goes further, charging Crumb with being in a state of "arrested juvenile development" and recommending that he "channel himself into doing better work."

That those most offended by Crumb's cartoons are female obviously raises larger questions about the relation between gender and aesthetic offense and why the experience is typically more distressing for women than for men (though certainly not for all women). As we see, the feminist position is explicitly aligned with the enterprise of sublimation and thus, presumably, with whatever forms of authority—psychical or social—mobilize its operations and its censorships. There are many reasons to object to this. But for me, the salience of these objections, and English's comments in particular, is the imperative to "Grow up." In other words, childhood is the origin of adult vulgarity. Rather than the usual clichéd island of innocence, for English, and also for filmmaker Zwigoff as we'll see, it's childhood that corrupts adulthood rather than the other way around. This is not exactly the conventional line at the moment, and therefore it's worth some attention.

Terry Zwigoff's *Crumb* isn't the story of Robert Crumb alone; it's also the story of Crumb's two brothers, Charles and Maxim, all three of whom are portrayed in extensive interviews. Zwigoff, who'd known the family for two decades, achieves something remarkably intimate in these scenes. Cartooning was, we learn, something of a childhood mania for all the brothers, who were abnormally close. Additionally all three shared and continue to share similar preoccupations with sex and aggression, although Charles, the eldest, has never actually *had* sex because he's too depressed to leave the house. Of the three brothers, Robert is the only one who can actually function in the world. Charles, who has never worked, has lived at home with his deeply strange mother since getting out of high school; he's heavily medicated and has attempted suicide numerous times, including once by drinking furniture polish. Maxim lives in a Single Room Occupancy and continues to paint (some of his work is stylistically not unlike Robert's) while practicing various of the more grisly Eastern-inflected bodily disciplines: meditating while sitting on a board of nails and swallowing lengths of cord that make their way through his intestinal tract. Apparently he makes a living by begging; he's also been arrested for, and readily admits to, molesting women on the street. Robert himself is inclined toward infantilism and various other fetishes; he's described by various women in a position to know as not "normal" in sexual relations, preferring pornography more than sex with another person and most of all masturbating to his own drawings. Nevertheless, he's now married with a young daughter, a late concession to conventional heterosexuality.

Still, in the world of the film, Robert might well pass for one of his strange hypersexual cartoon characters. At the same time, if it weren't for the cartoons, Robert might well have turned into one of his unfortunate mentally ill brothers: the film opens with him saying that when he doesn't draw he starts getting crazy and suicidal. Which is to say that the brothers, the cartoons, and Robert share some sort of essential nature: all seem to spring from the same origin; as the film unfolds, all the brothers start seeming like incarnations of Robert's demented cartoons. They themselves more or less say so: all are alarmingly articulate and mordantly funny about their various disorders. Nothing here is exactly repressed or unknown: the main difference between Robert and the other two is that for Charles and Maxim, the preoccupations with sex and aggression have been disabling in ultimately catastrophic ways; only Robert has been able to escape the brothers' fates by channeling these preoccupations into the content of the art. Not so for Charles, unfortunately: an epilogue informs us that he finally succeeded in committing suicide shortly after production was completed, and the film is dedicated to him.

The first thing to note about the structure of this film is that it stages the examination of Crumb's work in the context of a familiar genre, the artist biography; the second thing to note is that the current incarnation of the artist biography is the family story. The contradiction in this case is that Crumb's standing as an "artist" per se is, or should be, liminal—after all, he's a cartoonist, a genre with an uncertain footing in relation to the fine arts, traditionally speaking, though of course its stock has risen considerably in recent times, particularly in the years since *Crumb* was released. There's greater cultural respect for the cartoon form now than there's ever been, no doubt due to the emergence of culturally ambitious cartoonists such as Art Spiegelman, author of the Pulitzer Prize–winning *Maus,* taking on politically and culturally weighty matters in graphic form, a newly elevated standing to which this compelling portrait of a tormented cartoonist no doubt contributed. Crumb's own cultural status has shifted in the interim too, from a counterculture to a mainstream figure: he's now featured regularly in the *New Yorker* and other respectable venues.

There are many things to say about the shifting cultural fortunes of cartooning within the social hierarchy of cultural forms, and I can say only a few of them here. But if the rise and fall of different genres and styles is, as literary theorists like to suggest, part of a larger story about shifting modes and requirements for social subjectivities—the eighteenth-century invention of the novel was accompanied by a new focus on interior life and self-examination; modernist fragmentation mirrored conditions of increasing social anomie, and so on—then the question we'd obviously want to ask is what the heightened cultural status of cartooning says about the conditions of subjectivity at present. I'd argue that such shifts are what the film *Crumb* both evidences and in turn reproduces, precisely by treating Robert Crumb's work as the byproduct of an artistic subjectivity, rather than that of a sub-artistic hack or an industrial enterprise. Even now not all genres qualify for entry into the conventions of "auteurdom": you wouldn't expect to come across a biography of Danielle Steele, for example, though one of the things that the postmodern breakdown of distinctions between high and low cultural forms means is that fewer and fewer genres and figures *don't* qualify.

The artist biography is a genre that doesn't receive much critical attention, certainly not from film theorists; in fact even art historical treatments are rare. The first such treatment, published in 1934, is still one of the only historical surveys of print biographies; though brief, it spans ancient to modern times. The author was Ernst Kris, an art historian–psychoanalyst and follower of Freud, though Kris broke from Freud in taking the figure of the artist as a social construct, a cultural image produced precisely through the sorts of biographical texts that comprised his survey. Kris was something of a proto-structuralist: his approach was to break these biographies down into constitutive narrative units, or "primitive cells," and the basic narrative unit to be analyzed was what he called "the artist anecdote."[2] Through these anecdotes, which he collected and typologized, he believed it was possible to understand how the figure of the artist was being socially constructed in any given period. But it's also tempting to read Kris in reverse, to read these artist biographies for the descriptions they provide of the specific social *requirements* of the artist-hero figure at different points in history. Though Kris himself doesn't make the point, it's clear that artist biographies are written—and rewritten—to suit the requirements and norms of an age: Picasso used to be iconically life affirming and lusty; then he was a misogynist; no doubt soon he'll be queer.

What, then, comprises the current biographical formulae, the current required artist traits? In *Crumb*, although there's no voice-over performing explanation and exposition, a narrative is written nonetheless through the montage, the *mise-en-scène*, and the direction of the scenes. And where Crumb is directed, for much of the film, is back to his childhood, directed there literally in pilgrimages to the family domicile as well as though journeys of introspection and childhood reminiscence. But where else would he go, we contemporaries would doubtless ask. So habituated are we to this biographical formula that it seems entirely inevitable, though it's worth remembering that in other periods the biographical cells would have been entirely different. The classical conception of the role of the artist emphasized the continuities between generations, and so did the classical biographical cells; modernist formulae emphasized the breaking of ranks and oedipal conflicts. In our time, some form of familial or childhood trauma necessarily occupies the normative biographic cell; something is being "worked out" in the art, according to the typical artist anecdote.

At least the Crumb biopic leads us to this inference, given how many scenes portray the subject not just as a misanthropic social and sexual misfit, but as an artist whose work is an extension of the family scene. By juxtaposing "biographical units" of the tragic misfit brothers and their collective childhood cartoons with Crumb's adult cartoons—the visual similarities are unmistakable—any disjunction between family pathology and Crumb's subsequent career all but vanishes. Montage sequences and audio bridges tie the brothers' sexual preoccupations to Robert's oeuvre, focused largely on bizarre forms of sex and aggression carried out by a depressed band of perverse, lascivious, and highly physically endowed cartoon characters. The fact that Maxim has been convicted of real sex offenses—he likes to waylay women on the street and yank down their shorts, a compulsion he describes in alarming detail—retroactively transforms Robert's Mr. Natural into a fourth Crumb brother.

The film has an engaging lightness of tone even when telling this tragic tale. I'm not quarreling with the depiction—it's hard to dispute that something very bad happened to these three brothers along the way, possibly at the hands of a tyrannical authoritarian father—"the old man," the brothers call him—along with their pill-head, enema-wielding mother; some kind of horrific collective trauma that shaped and ordered Crumb's subsequent artwork. It also seems indisputable, on the evidence of the film, that the artist's childhood and the subsequent art are in continuity, though of course we're offered no competing ways of understanding Crumb's trajectory. To be sure, positing continuities between art and self aren't the preoccupation of our age alone: the madness of the artist and the suffering artist are familiar Romantic tropes. What seems recent is the way that biography has become so transparent, virtually identical with the artwork itself. Transformation, sublimation, what used to be called *aufhebung*—all eliminated. What remains is the landscape of trauma.

If, as Kris speculated, each era selects a new set of heroic characteristics for its artists to embody, if certain types of personalities rise in prominence due to the specificities and requirements of the moment, it's clear that the residues of childhood trauma have particular cultural resonance in our particular moment. You have only to track the meteoric rise of the abuse memoir in literary culture, its ubiquity as a talk-show topic and a cinematic theme: society has declared a state of emergency on the issue. The figure of the traumatized child has some sort of emotional hook for us, one that past generations were far less hooked by. The concept of abuse colors our perception of the world and now hovers uncomfortably over all adult–child relations.

This makes it particularly interesting that the criticism leveled by one of Crumb's most cogent (and offended) feminist critics is that "he's in a state of arrested juvenile development." Far from disagreeing with her, the filmmakers embrace this view of Crumb's work themselves; in fact, it's what confirms Crumb's status as an artist. The backdrop of trauma is what gives the work its authenticity: the fact that the work offends is a sign of its artistic merit. In another sequence juxtaposed with denunciations by feminist critics, noted art critic Robert Hughes compares Crumb to great artists of the past, like Goya, who employ disturbingly violent imagery. Thus certified by Hughes, there can be no doubt that Crumb is a qualified subject for the artist biography treatment we're watching—a treatment that in turn authenticates his standing as a real artist.

For Freud too, as for Crumb's feminist critics, the real artist was something of a schooled primitive: "a man who turns away from reality because he cannot come to terms with the renunciation of instinctual satisfaction . . . and who allows his erotic and ambitious wishes full play in the life of fantasy . . . but who because of his special gifts [is able to] mold his fantasies into truths of a new kind."[3] Yet for Freud, direct encounters with "the full play of fantasy," or the unmediated primitive, are impossible desires for the modern socialized subject, an impossibility that accounts for why the theme of the primitive resonates throughout his own work as well. No doubt the postmodern theorist will want to insert a proviso into the discussion reminding us that the category of the primitive is itself an invention of modernity and its obsession with development, which was exactly why it became such a source of fascination for so many adjacent turn-of-the-twentieth-century inventions, from psychoanalysis, to modernist aesthetics, to anthropology, all of which compulsively circle around this fateful dialectic. Despite all the sophisticated indictments of the colonial mentality in subsequent years, they haven't managed to eliminate developmental metaphors, which are deeply embedded in how we see and perceive the world. It may just be impossible to think without them.

The effects of these impossible-to-eliminate categories on visual perception is a theme that anthropologist Claude Lévi-Strauss ponders quite eloquently in his travelogue-memoir *Triste Tropique* (from which I crib my own essay's title), complaining: "I am subject to a double infirmity: all that I perceive offends me, and I constantly reproach myself for not seeing as much as I should."[4] The context is the aesthetic offense Lévi-Strauss suffers when witnessing spectacles of uneven development during his anthropological forays, that is, the conglomeration of the vanishing primitive and the encroaching modern in the same place. He doesn't mind spanking new suburbs or bricked-over cities: he's not simply or romantically anti-development. But he wants it to be all or nothing, savage or suburb; the conjunctions of the two stymies him, inducing a refusal—or, as he fears, a failure—to *see* what's actually there, even as it's disappearing under development's wrecking ball. But there's nothing to do about it: to be a modern means that the simultaneous presence of different levels of development simply *offends,* and this is, according to Lévi-Strauss, the foundation of modern perception.

If the primitive is a category invented by moderns, so too is regression a category invented by adults. This problem of uneven development is also, as we know, the founding problem of psychoanalysis, though not one so easily cured either. Freud's entire account of the perceptual system, which he begins outlining in *Interpretation of Dreams,* rests on the premise of uneven development: not only is regular nightly regression in the form of dreams a firmly entrenched aspect of normal subjectivity, but normal waking perception itself is founded on a regressive foundation, because attention is always put into motion by something *prior,* something from the past. In other words, attention is a state that *revives* something for the perceiving subject; it revisits something already there. There are no new perceptions in this account—there can't be: all we have are the shadows and traces of long-lost objects and desires. An experience of humiliation, to take a random example (except that by this logic there are no random examples), is a form of attention in which a pathway to an old source of emotion is traversed, and "as soon as the memory of it is touched, it springs into life once again and shows itself cathected with excitation."[5] Paying attention isn't a *choice*—nor is being offended—they're dictated to us by the past. Thus the most intense forms of attention—anger, love, aesthetic offense— are constructed like memorials, and for that reason they have higher degrees of psychical intensity, often described with metaphors of distance and proximity: they seem "closer." For Freud, as for Lévi-Strauss, the dialectic between progression and regression, the simultaneous presence of relics and the new, and the various journeys this entails—dreams, anthropological voyages, or those undertaken on the psychoanalyst's couch—are the fundaments of modern perception.

We return now from these side trips and peregrinations to our current case study. *Crumb* offers some interesting updates on the old motifs. To begin with, it draws heavily on the currently popular theme of childhood trauma as an absent cause. In these case, it's positioned as causal in the formation of the creative drive—not just an origin, but also a reparation. The question we might want to ask in this context is whether the motif of childhood trauma, so insistently present in our culture at the moment—in culture, in the humanities and social sciences—is the reappearance of the primitive in a new guise, our generation's update on the theme? Functionally speaking, childhood trauma and an older notion of the primitive play similar roles, preserving and retaining uneven levels of development within the same temporality—or in our case, within the same subjectivity. Trauma becomes an artifact to be preserved and memorialized, and this is especially so to the degree it provides the unconscious wellsprings for artistic production, just as geographic versions of primitivism did for early-twentieth-century modernists. If the primitive locales were once located in colonial outposts, exterior rather than subjective and interiorized, let's recall that the interior–exterior distinction was never entirely so rock solid either: the so-called heart of darkness was always one of modernism's big themes.

Needless to say, trauma narratives aren't new when it comes to cultural production; human suffering has a long history. What seems different at the moment is the attenuation of the old literary and visual codes through which those themes were deployed, the decline of transformation and sublimation as necessary steps in cultural production. For Freud, sublimation was the cultural and aesthetic *solution* to traumas of the past, though sublimation is a concept with a somewhat tangled status in psychoanalytic thought. The basic theory, as is well known, posits that socially and psychically unacceptable goals—sexual or aggressive, primitive wishing and desiring—are transformed into acceptable goals or "higher purposes." But sublimation supposedly also involves a second process, the neutralization of the contents of those goals or injuries, to the point that they become unrecognizable, losing their reference to the original material. In the old model, aesthetic experience is a sort of encoding-decoding operation, occasioned by the meeting of two distinct subjectivities—author and reader, artist and viewer—with the aesthetic forming a sort of bridge from one unconscious to another. The disguised, sublimated material brought to bear by the artist or writer resonates unconsciously with the disguised, sublimated instincts of the reader or viewer, producing frisson and pleasure. This is what comprises "aesthetic experience"—a re-encounter with split-off, dangerously primitive materials and wishes. What we're encountering are our own deepest renounced selves.

Interestingly, in Freud's account of sublimation, to be overly absorbed with sexual themes, in the manner of the Crumb brothers, is a symptom of "compulsive brooding, in a distorted and unfree form."[6] In contrast, the creativity of sublimation is the *escape route*, from both sexual repression and a neurotic compulsive thinking about sexual themes. Whether this is merely Freud's Victorianism speaking or a prescription for our own current sexual malaise is something we sexually enlightened postmoderns can certainly argue about. Another question to ask is whether it's facile (or overly optimistic) to conflate sexual explicitness with increased freedom, as sexual progressives would have it. As *Crumb* powerfully demonstrates, there's far less freedom in Crumb's work than strict adherence to old familial rules, which allow for these three beset brothers nothing *but* sexual brooding. It's clear to anyone with eyes to see that freedom is not exactly what's on display here.

Voicing this observation gives me no pleasure; I fear it pushes me toward the fuddy-duddy camp. To compound the problem, like Crumb's feminist critics, I admit to finding the Crumb family sensibility offensive, though I'm not sure it's precisely feminist offense I'm experiencing. To be honest, what I found myself most offended by while viewing the film, oddly enough, wasn't Robert Crumb's cartoons, but his *laugh*, which is disturbing and often wildly inappropriate. Robert giggles while Charles is talking about his suicide attempt, chortles while Max is talking about molesting women, and sniggers at just about every point in which the emotional content is pain and tragedy. The camerawork in the film is brilliant, always panning quickly to Crumb at such moments, which is to say the camera itself provides the "biographical anecdotes" in these instances, so attentive to the cartoonist's distorted affect that Crumb soon begins to seem like a continuation of his lewd cartoon characters, and they of him. He begins to seem like a caricature of himself.

The regulation of behavior is the fundamental project of development, no doubt true whether we mean the development from primitive to modern, or from child to adult. According to psychologists, children progress from using the whole body as an apparatus for expression into the refinements of language, thought and speech, which are the modern subject's tools for mastering the world and making contact with the environment. Laughter is a more primitive form of expression, a residue left over from infancy and childhood when the entire body was used to signal pleasure and displeasure. In other words, you might call laughter a sanctioned form of regression, and very much a shared regression, a shared pleasure. Laughter is a profoundly social act; it solicits identification—people often start to laugh at another person's laughter without even knowing what they're laughing at.

And on other occasions they stop laughing. Solicitations to laughter can also invoke self-rebuke, the punishment of the ego. After all, social development is secured by a variety of brutal enforcement techniques—spankings, shame, and humiliation, to name just a few—which become internalized in the socialization process. With successful socialization, defying social proprieties and restrictions provokes painful self-reproach: we no longer need parents and society to punish our transgressions, since we do it ourselves. Such are the consequences of development.

I was interested to observe in myself that Crumb's laugh provoked profound discomfort, so much so that I can only imagine it somehow activated this self-reproachful trigger. Like his feminist critics, the supposed humor of his antics failed to convince me; something aggressive and disturbing registered instead, something for which the laugh seems to be a bribe, a subterfuge. The inappropriate laugh is like a behavioral condensation of Crumb's visual aesthetic, both founded on the reversal of affect. And Crumb's "adult" cartoons do quite brilliantly condense these uneven developments: they're a perfect formal device, childish impulses and adult sexuality co-existing within every frame. Still, I too, like Crumb's critics, wish he would "grow up" and leave regression behind, would stop memorializing those painful relics, whose traces in this thwarted and unevenly developed grown-up are so unsettling—exactly because they're so recognizable to anyone who was once a child. What refuge is there from this recognition? Aesthetic offense at least removes one from the distressing scene of identification and protects against the self-reproaches such identifications might incite.

But it wasn't only Crumb's laugh that unsettled me, frankly, it was his very physiognomy; in fact the physiognomy of the whole family is unsettling. In the early childhood photos the family looks fairly conventional in appearance, but as they get older, the three sons get uglier and uglier, with distorted features and odd, inappropriate affect. It's as though they've *all* become self-caricatures, as if their bodies had provided a pliant medium upon which to record some particularly grotesque story, a story that language alone was insufficiently plastic to express.

Caricature is a peculiar genre. Historically it's been a form in which artists employ techniques of distortion to show the true essence of a person behind the thin pretense of social convention. As Ernst Kris observes, it made a surprisingly late appearance on the aesthetic scene, only fully surfacing in the sixteenth century, despite the fact that all of the technical skills required were certainly available far earlier. Some new degree of social permissibility must have been the preconditions for its emergence, he speculates, the lifting of some previous form of self-censorship in psychical and social aggression. Kris views caricature as a mixture of regression and aggression: it's a deliberate distortion of the features of a person for the purposes of mockery, thus as much of a psychological mechanism as a mode of art. As he puts it, "The carica-turist seeks for the perfect deformity, he shows how the soul of the man would express itself in his body if only matter were sufficiently pliable to nature's intentions."[7]

When it comes to the Crumb brothers, it appears that their bodies were indeed sufficiently pliable to advertise the damage to their souls, at least according to the aesthetic evidence on display. The Crumb oeuvre too, clearly encumbered by the same familial phantasmatic (a term that psychoanalyst Jean Laplanche uses to describe the core struc-turing action, the *mise-en-scène*, that shapes and orders any individual psychical life), also deploys caricature as its medium of mockery, solic-iting our laughter. But how funny *are* these encumbrances—is this a joke we want to be in on? One of the reasons I find it so difficult to take an unambivalent position on obscenity—to champion it as a form of free expression and take pleasure in its license (which at some intel-lectual level I do also applaud)—is the suspicion that, as in the case of the Crumb aesthetic, there's always more to the story, some subterfuge about origins. Obscenity isn't just a matter of the obscene content, after all; it's also a particular sort of form: a repetition, the compulsive return to a scene. Something's being revisited, memorialized, though most of the time we don't know what. This seems to be the lesson of *Crumb:* the pleasures of the obscene are also a kind of misdirection, an inducement not to look at what can't be named.

If "freedom of expression" is the progressive's slogan in debates about obscenity, it would be an excessively optimistic slogan to employ here: there's nothing particularly "free" about Crumb's work, not if we mean freedom in the largest sense of the word, in the social *and* psychi-cal senses. And shouldn't that be what we're striving for? If those of us who study obscenity are so busy championing it that we forget to notice what's offensive about it, we're missing the point, I think.

Notes

1. "The Career Couch," *New York Times* February 18, 2007.

2. Ernst Kris, *Psychoanalytic Explorations in Art* (New York: International Universities Press, 1952), 64–84.

3. Sigmund Freud, "Formulations on the Two Principles of Mental Functioning" (1911). Translated and reprinted in *Standard Edition*, vol. 12 (London: Hogarth: 1961), 244.

4. Claude Lévi-Strauss, *Tristes Tropiques,* trans. John and Doreen Weightman (New York: Penguin, 1992), 43.

5. Sigmund Freud, *Interpretation of Dreams* (1900). Translated and reprinted in *Standard Edition*, vol. 4 (London: Hogarth: 1961), 88.

6. Sigmund Freud, "Leonardo da Vinci and a Memory of His Childhood," trans. James Strachey (New York: W. W. Norton, 1964), 29.

7. Kris, 177–90.

Pecunia Olet

Affluence, Effluence, and Obscenity

> *One tends to see only the thousand tricks of power which are enacted*
> *above ground; but these are the least part of it. Underneath, day in,*
> *day out, is digestion and again digestion.*
>
> —*Elias Canetti,* Crowds and Power

One of us (Mikita) comes from England, and we begin this essay with a
recollection from her childhood:

> When I was about eight years old, I went to a sleepover at the home
> of my playmate, the vicar's daughter. I didn't know it at the time, but
> her family was rich. When we were in bed at night, just before going to
> sleep, my friend's mother came to the door and asked if either of us
> would like to "spend a penny" before going to sleep. I got out of bed,
> took some coins from my jeans pocket, and followed the vicar's wife
> down the hall. I don't know what I expected, but I was surprised to dis-
> cover that she was merely leading me to the toilet. This was possibly my
> first introduction to the strong cultural connection between money and
> bodily excretion.

In its negative form, this cultural association is often attributed to
Vespasian, the first-century emperor who gave Rome its first public pay
toilets. When his son Titus criticized the idea, Vespasian replied that
the "urine tax" would redound to the good of the city, and that even

130

though it may originate in the toilet, money doesn't stink: "*Pecunia non olet.*" American readers may know this phrase from Robert Penn Warren's novel *All the King's Men,* where narrator Jack Burden quotes it.[1] But we'll be making the case that only in Utopia (Thomas More's *Utopia,* that is) are the chamber pots made of gold. Money does stink—"*pecunia olet*"—and some kinds of money stink more than others.

Spending a penny

Everybody is familiar with terms like "filthy lucre" and "cash" that needs "laundering," and many of us know somebody who is "rolling in it" or is "stinking rich." According to Sigmund Freud, it's natural to associate money with dirt, because that's what money is: shit. Or at least that's what it's like. "In reality," wrote Freud in 1908, "wherever archaic modes of thought have predominated or still persist—in the ancient civilizations, in myths, fairy tales and superstitions, in unconscious thinking, in dreams and in neuroses—money is brought into the most intimate relationship with dirt," adding that "the gold which the devil gives his paramours turns into excrement after his departure" and that "everyone is familiar with the 'shitter of ducats.'"[2] In a 1911 essay, Freud and Ernst Oppenheim quote a scholar's observation that "gold, according to ancient oriental mythology, is the excrement of hell.[3] In a 1914 case history, Freud stressed that an interest in accumulating money is libidinal rather than rational in character, relating this to the child's ability to hold back shit or to produce it as his or her first symbolic offering.[4] And the flip side of accumulation, expenditure, has the same inherent set of meanings, as philosopher Georges Bataille averred when he said that ceremonial gift-giving "symbolizes excretion, which itself is linked to death."[5]

These ideas were vividly elaborated by Freud's colleague Sandor Ferenczi, who wrote in 1914 that feces held back "are really the first 'savings' of the growing being, and as such remain in a constant, unconscious inter-relationship with every bodily activity or mental striving that has anything to do with collecting, hoarding, and saving."[6] Ferenczi expands on Freud's observation that as children become acculturated they start finding shit unpleasant and begin collecting other things—first pieces of bodily detritus such as hair and toenails, then external items such as stones, marbles, and buttons. When even these objects start offending the child's sense of hygiene and something still purer is demanded, the commonly found answer is—shining pieces of money.

Money itself can be further purified, moreover, since the greater the sum of money collected, the more abstract it becomes. Shining coins that you can run through your hands, pile up, and jingle in your pocket become bank notes. Bank notes are objects too, and it feels good to see them bulging out of your pay packet, to press them into a wad in your wallet, to lick your fingers and pull one out. In the next stage, however, the bank notes become checks, credit cards, and finally pure symbolism, nothing more than figures on a printout from a bank or financial institution—so much in, so much out—or impulses in an electronic ledger, intangible units of information on a screen.

Still, money *qua* money retains its age-old connection with the unclean. For a vivid expression of this in popular culture, one need look no further than the films of Alfred Hitchcock, who repeatedly invokes the link between money and shit. At the beginning of *Shadow of a Doubt,* made in 1943, Hitchcock signals that the seemingly benign Uncle Charlie is actually a psychopath by showing fistfuls of cash spilled over his bedside table and onto the floor. In the 1972 thriller *Frenzy,* a serial rapist and murderer must retrieve a piece of jewelry from a corpse stowed on a potato truck, which deposits its load onto the street like a lumbering beast with diarrhea. The most striking example appears in the 1960 masterpiece *Psycho,* where a large amount of money, stolen by Janet Leigh's character, is equated with shit in startling and explicit ways. After the theft she imagines her victims discussing the loot in scatological double entendres: "She sat there while I dumped it out," says the businessman who pulled the money from his pocket and then flaunted it in front of her like a naughty boy proud of the excrement he's "made." Later she enters a lavatory to handle the cash, and later still she takes a piece of paper and calculates how much of the money she has spent, and then flushes the paper down a toilet, prompting Hollywood's first-ever close-up of a flushing toilet. The money eventually winds up in the trunk of her car, which the film's eponymous psycho (played by Anthony Perkins) sinks in a nearby swamp, metaphorically pictured by Hitchcock as a toilet writ large, especially when the car momentarily refuses to sink politely out of sight—every toilet flusher's nightmare! Other examples, in works by Hitchcock and other filmmakers, are easy to come by.

Freud himself couldn't ask for better instances of sublimated shit in the popular imagination. What these visual tropes have in common is their adherence to the classic definition of dirt as matter out of place—here it's money and other valuables that have been wrenched from their proper locations—and to Mary Douglas's observation that dirt "offends against order," since here metaphorical dirt is used to signify the presence of deeply disordered minds.[7] Also relevant to this imagery is Jean-Paul Sartre's concept of the obscene as that which "appears when the body adopts postures which entirely strip it of its acts and which reveal the inertia of its flesh. . . . [I]t is *de trop*. . . . [It] "releases to me the inert expanding of flesh . . . when I am not in a state of desire for this flesh . . . ."[8] A standard dictionary definition of obscene is "so excessive as to be offensive," and if we apply Sartre's evocation of "inert expanding" to money, it provides a useful illustration of how "*pecunia olet*" may pertain to the very rich. We of the less-privileged classes would certainly desire what the super-rich have if there weren't *more of* what they have than we can readily get our minds around. Through its enormity—in both senses of the word—the wealthy person's money loses shape, becoming an amorphous monster, a metastasized doppelgänger of the *reasonable* degree of wealth that we could easily conceptualize and covet. Piles of money are a benison. Mountains of money are scary.

Psychoanalysts often place attitudes to money along a spectrum. At one pole is the compulsive spender, who gets rid of everything he earns and more. In the spirit of Bataille, we call this the excremental personality. At the other pole is the hoarder, who lives far beneath her income and refuses to part with a penny. This is the anal personality, and the adjective fits all too well. Ferenczi observed many cases in which "people are economical [i.e., stingy] as regards the changing of under-linen [i.e., underpants] in a way quite out of proportion to their standard of living in other respects."[9]

The first is the excremental personality; the second is the anal-retentive type. Having begun our discussion with the English practice of "spending a penny," we'll mention at this point our curiosity as to whether the anal personality's extreme economies might also pertain to the British desire to cling to the pound at all costs, refusing to give it up and switch over to the Euro, as has happened in other countries. Should we see this as an attempt to keep the island clean, uncontaminated by Continental effluvia? Does it have any relation to the fact that, according to telegraph.co.uk, each person in England uses thirty-nine pounds of toilet paper per annum, which comes to 110 rolls per capita, some two-and-a-half times the European average?

All money is dirty; some money is obscene

It appears to us that the adjective "obscene" has been used with increasing frequency in recent years to describe extremely large amounts of money. There are many examples, but one well-known usage in popular culture is heard in the 1990 film *Pretty Woman,* where the corporate raider played by Richard Gere tells a fawning boutique assistant that he'd better prepare to grovel cravenly before his prostitute girlfriend, played by Julia Roberts, because they plan to spend "an obscene amount of money" in the store.

In phrases like "dirty money" and "filthy lucre," the cash is what's unclean, not the possessor of it; and, even then, it doesn't literally crawl with vermin or stink of excretions. Describing an amount of money as "obscene" is a more literal use of language, because the word "obscene" carries a weight of moral disapproval that goes beyond a lack of cleanliness, and is necessarily aimed at whoever has accumulated the undue quantity. The stain of obscenity is more difficult to remove than the stain of dirt, since it seems to bleed over to the person who receives the money, the deal, or the offer, and who then becomes contaminated by this contact.

The pace of change triggered by recent technological advances, such as dot-com and digital technologies, has radically transformed how people acquire wealth. Traditionally, great wealth was something you were born into or inherited from your family. It's long been possible for people who aren't born rich to make their own fortunes, of course— the *nouveaux riches* are virtually as old as the *anciens riches*—but historically this has usually been a long, hard process. There is little precedent for the speed at which people today, including very young people, can get incredibly wealthy. This quickness of acquisition often makes those who become suddenly rich more aware of their wealth than might have been the case if they'd been eased into their new socioeconomic status, which offers marked contrasts with their former standards of living, and also with the poverty of others. The newly rich may therefore have an impression that their large quantities of money are out of place in the sense of being unevenly or improperly distributed, and excessive in the sense of being more than the formerly middle- or working-class individual readily understands how to use in ways that will be effective and gratifying in the long run. And, as we've noted, being out of place and excessive are the twin essences of obscenity.

We typed the phrase "obscene amount of money" into *Google* on 3 December 2007 and, excluding some personal and business blogs, the first ten results were:

(1) The listing for *Washington on $10 Million a Day: How Lobbyists Plunder the Nation,* a book by Ken Silverstein, on Amazon.com.

(2) A news article from the *New York Times* discussing the $25 million

that Barack Obama's campaign took in during the first fund-raising season of the 2008 presidential race.

(3) Another article from the *New York Times* declaring that a Virginia governor had raised millions of dollars for a possible presidential bid.

(4) A news item from bbc.co.uk reporting that a £500,000 donation from a wealthy businessman enabled a Scottish political party to exceed its fundraising target of £1 million.

(5) A post on Drug WarRant.com about a United States plan to help Mexico fight drug trafficking at a projected cost of up to $1.2 billion over three years.

(6) A post on Yahoo! Answers asking if soccer star David Beckham will be worth the "obscene amount of money" he's receiving.

(7) A post on Limos.com reporting that an electronics company had announced a loss of $59 billion over a three-month period, and wondering how one enterprise could lose such an "obscene" amount.

(8) An item in *Domain's Magazine* stating that the investment of obscene sums by zealous venture capitalists was the "most astounding thing" about the dot-com boom of the late 1990s and early 2000s.

(9) A blog post about Beckham, reporting that in 2007 he would sign with the Los Angeles Galaxy for £128 million, or $250 million, over five years, giving him a weekly salary of almost $1 million.

(10) An item in *The Australian* saying that the nation's two largest advertisers, both of which spent "an obscene amount of money" on messages to the public, "are a company now in much financial trouble and the federal government, which spent almost $600,000 a day on a single campaign, not counting the cost of producing the ads."

These examples have a number of common elements:

(1) The sums are enormous, ranging up to many billions of dollars.

(2) Political money and government spending are dominant subjects.

(3) Attention largely centers on enormous sums going to one person (e.g., a candidate for public office) or to one industry (e.g., dot-com companies) even though the money could be more effectively used with more efficient distribution patterns.

(4) The sums are often spent or collected in ways that don't produce anything tangible, only ephemeral things like the buzz of an election campaign or the services of a fashionable athlete.

(5) Most of these references relate not to long-established pillars of the financial and political worlds but to individuals and organizations connected with new money, i.e., money that's given or accrued with much greater speed and in vastly larger amounts than would have happened in similar cases in earlier times.

Old money may also be unfairly distributed, to be sure, but since the inequities of dynastic wealth have been around long enough for denizens of a capitalist society to grow accustomed to them, they attract less interest and less contentiousness. What feels obscene is the perception that "our" money—as citizens, customers, investors, or residents of places more fortunate than New Orleans—is going to someone who doesn't seem to deserve it and certainly doesn't need it. Given the levels of poverty and need in the U.S. and elsewhere, it seems obscene that any one person should receive hugely disproportionate amounts of money, especially a person who is already rich. The same goes for institutions that don't make manifestly strong contributions to the public good. Think of the belated attention being given by some American commentators and legislators, after years of delay, to the waste of prodigious sums in Iraq, much of it showered on the likes of Halliburton and unaccountable private contractors via noncompetitive contracts and unaudited dispersals.

While it's interesting to see which particular instances of vast and underserved wealth strike average people as exceptionally offensive, it's still difficult to explain why these over-the-top expenditures so readily exude the distinctive odor of obscenity. After all, the money that's paid to people like Beckham or Washington lobbyists isn't taken away from the rest of us, at least not directly. On the contrary, given how much tax people with huge salaries are required to pay, they may create as much wealth as they keep for themselves—if they actually pay the taxes, that is, or if their tax dodges are worthy charities of the kind to which, say, Bill and Melinda Gates contribute. So where does the popular disgust come from? If it's not our money, and it isn't illegally earned, why do we consider it obscene?

One answer comes from folklore scholar Alan Dundes, who explains this phenomenon in relation to the superstition—common in both ancient and modern societies—that there is a limited amount of good in the world, and therefore gain for one person can come only at the expense of another.[10] According to this belief, enormous profits in one place will be offset by enormous loss elsewhere. We're each allocated our fair share of the world's good, so if *you* get lucky, it means somebody *else,* somewhere, is getting cheated or short-changed.

Dundes argues that the notion of "limited good" also explains the common practice of "downplaying" one's possessions in public: the removal of price tags from gifts; customs that forbid eating in front of others without inviting them to join in, especially in countries where many people are chronically hungry; and all the other social taboos against flaunting one's wealth the way, for example, the *Psycho* businessman does. Consider the social injunctions in modern societies against asking someone how much he paid for something, or how much she earns; alluding to such matters outside a strictly business context is socially risky except between the closest friends, and naming specific figures is considered downright gauche. We've all seen movies where, even when there's nobody else around, a person doing business doesn't name a figure but instead jots the number on a piece of paper and hands it to the second party, like a magic word that can't be spoken aloud without breaking the spell. The matters shrouded by such strangely secretive customs—the questions that shouldn't be asked, the subjects that shouldn't be raised, the words that shouldn't be spoken—reveal, by the very fact of their enshrouding, close connections to the bodily functions they represent and intertwine with in the unconscious. Issues related to the toilet and the wallet, we discover early on, share two qualities that are conjoined so thoroughly and persistently in few other areas of life: They are ubiquitous, integral to every individual's everyday experience, and they are hypersensitive, demanding to be approached with scrupulous tact and discretion if they must be approached at all. The presence of excrement as an ingredient in many love potions, writes philosopher of art Allen S. Weiss, points to a "scatological eroticism, a remnant of primal symbolizations where the potentially dangerous excreta is transformed into a magical good object" linked to "powers of potency and omnipotence."[11] As a similarly robust aphrodisiac, money partakes of similar magic. No wonder we require both of these dynamic forces to hide their prodigious powers behind veils of dissimulation and denial.

A comparable insight comes from Elias Canetti, who provides literature's most unyielding description of the intimacy with which money, power, and shit are bound together. In the relationship it demands with the person who produces it, Canetti writes, "excrement belongs to the sphere of power. . . . The constant pressure which, during the whole of its long progress through the body, is applied to the prey which has become food . . . may very well be seen as the central, if most hidden, process of power," closely linked to the practice of dominating others by sucking away their substance with an all-consuming greed for treasure and dominance, and then disposing of them "as he does of his excrement, simply seeing to it that they do not poison the air of his house."[12] To those whose moral sensibilities or psychic inhibitions constrict the exercise and dampen the exhilaration of such power, or withhold free access to their allotted share, the forces of this excremental power must certainly seem dark, dangerous, obscene.

It is clear that the superstitions attaching to money and shit, the agents of possession and dispossession, retain great implicit power in our allegedly enlightened time. And the superstitions most likely to have such staying power are those that contain some degree of commonly accepted truth. The belief that one person's comfort comes at the hidden expense of others' suffering is one of these. Any unreconstructed Marxist will tell you this, and so will the many conservatives who buy into the limited-good hypothesis on selected occasions—not when excessive wealth is in question, but when hard-to-measure ideological values such as "freedom" and "liberty" are at stake. Defending his right-wing view of limited government at his failed confirmation hearing for a Supreme Court appointment, for instance, Robert Bork asserted that any law providing a freedom for one person or group necessarily subtracts a freedom from some other person or group—a position that infuriated less constipated thinkers, who responded with the reverse argument that a liberty for one is a liberty for all.

These are oversimplifications, to be sure; exceptions and hard cases abound, since in the diffuse arena of worldly satisfaction magnitudes and comparisons must be subjectively felt rather than impartially computed. Yet the limited-good perspective has proven to be an enduring aspect of the popular unconscious, partly because it satisfies two bedrock psychological traits of the modern and pre-modern subject: the (narcissistic) desire to see other people's excessively or inappropriately accrued wealth as an unjust subtraction from the equivalent affluence to which we ourselves are rightly entitled, and the (sadomasochistic) need to perceive our own limited means as worthy of similar abhorrence by those even more deprived than we are. There is a powerful and eternal tie between the urge to acquire treasure and the urge to keep others away from it, and in this tie we find another echo of Freud's insight that for the developing subject in the sadistic-anal stage of development, obediently producing shit "for the sake of . . . someone else" is simultaneously a gratifying venture into the social order, grounded in the emerging sense of intersubjective exchange, and a bodily sacrifice felt as "a prototype of castration," grounded in the terrors of loss and lack.[13] It is no wonder that we love money with so much passion and fear its effects with so much anxiety.

And anxiety over worldly satisfaction does indeed run high, as Anton Chekhov eloquently recognizes at the end of "Gooseberries," a short story of 1898: "There ought to be behind the door of every happy, contented man someone standing with a hammer continually reminding him with a tap that there are unhappy people; that however happy he may be, life will show him her laws sooner or later, trouble will come for him—disease, poverty, losses, and no one will see or hear, just as now he neither sees nor hears others."[14]

The obscenely rich: A demoralized minority

Discomfort with money is deeply rooted. If your parents were shifty or ill at ease about money matters, you've probably picked up their anxieties, although you may not be consciously aware of it. Even for people who don't normally give money much thought, it's hard to escape the struggle to pick up the check after dinner in a restaurant, or the difficulties involved in buying gifts, or the discomfort that arises when a homeless person gets on your subway car and starts asking for money. Hardly anyone is immune, and the very rich are perhaps less immune than others.

Yes, as surprising as it may seem, we must pity the poor zillionaire. According to psychiatrist Peter A. Olsson, M.D., in an article called "Complexities in the Psychology and Psychotherapy of the Phenomenally Wealthy," those who are rolling in it suffer from the same levels of misery, angst, and depression as everyone else, and, in addition, they may find themselves beset by *special* problems of the filthy rich. Olsson explains how money, which easily translates into recognition, power, and entitlement, can often cause sensations of loneliness, entrapment, and isolation, as well as various neuroses—sociopathy, extreme narcissism, impaired identity formation, inner isolation, and others—plus weakened family structure and feelings of severe inadequacy.[15] Those who have made large fortunes through their own efforts may become addicted to a cycle of intense work, huge paychecks, high social status, and compulsive spending, with the downside of self-destructive behavior, immoderate vanity, and problems maintaining relationships. As for those who acquired extreme wealth by being born into it, psychologist Stephen Goldbart—cofounder of the Money, Meaning & Choices Institute—has found that they often need therapeutic help in coping with "the emotional complexities of having money" and negotiating the difficult transition "from emotional bankruptcy to emotional richness." Similar observations were made by John Sedgwick, who wrote in his 1985 book *Rich Kids: America's Young Heirs and Heiresses, How They Love and Hate Their Money,* that those who inherit great wealth may have feelings of guilt "more severe, and more permanent" than those of many actual criminals, who at least

> have something to confess. They can receive forgiveness, they can reform, they can put the sins behind them. But rich kids start to feel they are the sin themselves, and every crime that was ever committed now hangs on their heads. They see the inequity that lies about them, or read about it . . . and they think they are responsible for it. Because they are on top, they must be squashing those on the bottom. This is the true embarrassment of riches.[16]

Not every filthy-rich person is afflicted by psychological pains, to be sure, but the wealth-management industry has built a profitable sideline dedicated to helping the unlucky ones whose advantages are disadvantages, producing powerful guilt feelings and a consequent need to do penance, to suffer, and to hide their wealth from others, even from themselves.

For a high-profile instance of too much money inducing a sense of self-disgust, consider the case of Tom Monaghan, who built Domino's Pizza into a source of astonishing personal wealth. Monaghan is very religious, spending (or squandering) large quantities of money on ambitious projects related to the conservative Roman Catholicism in which he believes. In the early 1990s he radically reordered his priorities, according to *New Yorker* writer Peter J. Boyer, after a sudden, blinding realization that by accumulating great riches he had been indulging the sin of pride.[17] The very next day he began selling his earthly treasures—the house, the helicopter, the jet, the private island, the Detroit Tigers—many of them at a staggering loss. He subsequently sold Domino's for a cool $1 billion and consecrated all of his resources to church-related philanthropy, declaring, "I want to die broke." What interests us is neither the proximate cause nor the eventual outcome of Monaghan's life-changing decision, but rather the abruptness of its advent—he received his flash of insight, swore what he called a "millionaire's vow of poverty" in bed that very night, and began parting with his worldly goods the next morning—and the thoroughness with which he followed through on it; no loss was too immense to tolerate as long as the sale took place immediately and irrevocably. We diagnose this as a drastic case of *Pecunia Olet,* the filthy lucre disease, wherein the stench of obscene wealth grows so intensely nauseating to its owner that the impulse to purge it, regurgitate it, shit and piss it out becomes irresistible.

All of this said, Monaghan greatly enjoyed his years of wheeling and dealing, and he maintains a hands-on approach to his philanthropic endeavors. For him, as for most modern citizens, the accumulation and disposal of money—the first phase already accomplished in Monaghan's case, the second in progress for the foreseeable future—has become the standard way to measure a successful life, outstripping such traditional achievements as enjoying leisure, pursuing wisdom, and engaging in creative work outside the business world. As a result, financial success has become so confused with personal and psychological well-being that it's almost impossible to have wealth without feeling emotional conflict. (We grant, however, that Monaghan's wealth-generated anxieties may be tempered by his expectation of the ultimate golden parachute, a fast track to heaven after he shuffles off his gilded mortal coil.)

Those of us who lack excessive wealth may claim indifference toward those who have it, but most of us are envious as well as resentful; we indulge in unapologetic bias against the super-rich as a matter of principle, just as we sentimentalize those who claim to spurn money—starving artists, selfless humanitarians, and the like—and are jolted when they prove to be as vulnerable to money-related misery as the rest of us. Olsson presents research to demonstrate that the "phenomenally wealthy" are a dispirited minority, suffering the same problems as any other downtrodden group; yet it's hard not to find this claim ridiculous—a myth propagated by the rich, perhaps, to cheer up the rest of us and get us off their case. Merely to discuss the problems of the rich seems trivial, even ridiculous, compared to facing the problems of those discriminated against because of, say, race or poverty or sexuality. There's not much you can do about the color of your skin or the burden of your caste, but nobody ever had trouble getting rid of cash. After all, you can't take it with you.

Or can you?

Taking it with you

Money works because we all tacitly consent that it should; outside the boundaries of a given social system, that system's financial structures seem curious if not nonsensical. Yet money is everywhere, in one form or another, and systems that don't use "real" money develop their own currencies—think of communes, prisons, casinos, the board game Monopoly, the Internet game Second Life—that can in some cases be exchanged for "real" money. Money is so taken for granted that we easily forget it's only a signifier, a substitute, a representation. Money is the ultimate symbol, both everything and nothing, and this semiotically unstable entity, which doesn't even have to take a tangible form, can be the difference between life and death.

In his book *Escape from Evil*, cultural anthropologist Ernest Becker argues that, although we rarely acknowledge the fact, money has come to serve the ritual function of religion. Money is the most natural of gods; our belief in it, our conformity to its standards, simply goes without saying. If you don't conform to its laws, you will be severely punished, perhaps even executed; but if you accept its power, you can achieve eternal life, or a reasonable facsimile thereof. The capacity to transcend death, in fact, is the ultimate power that money shares with other gods. Monaghan the pizza king may be on to something after all.

Throughout history, Becker declares, humans have used and discarded "immortality symbols," representations of cosmic power and divinity.[18] Coins are physical mementos of these imagoes, or idealized mental images; the circular coin, for instance, represents the crown, the halo, and the orbs of sun and moon; banknotes bear the images of kings, presidents, and other heroes.[19] This indicates the profound role played by money rituals in our attempts to shore up defenses against the fear, helplessness, and dependency that terrify us in facing the inevitability of death. As philosopher Norman O. Brown wrote, "accumulations of stone and gold make possible the discovery of the immortal soul. . . . Death is overcome on condition that the real actuality of life pass into these immortal and dead things; money is the man; the immortality of an estate or a corporation resides in the dead things which alone endure."[20]

Today's immortality symbols take a more abstract form than gold under the floorboards or moneybags in the safe; now they take the form of wills, estates, memorials, and legacies. The psychoanalyst Otto Rank argued that religions, morals, customs, and laws represent limits we set on ourselves so we can transcend our human condition—denying life in order to get more life, to make ourselves immortal.[21] In this context, money represents sacrifice. The source of the English word "gold" is the Old German word "geld," which means "sacrifice" and is related, along with words like "gild" and "gilt," to the word "guilt." Until recently, banks were built to resemble sacrificial temples. Now, also like churches, they can take any form as long as they appear serious, safe, and generic; yet their unconscious links to the masochistic pleasure of sacrifice and the existential dread of castration remain in place. Accordingly, the presence of all that money requires a respectful hush; you don't sit and chat in a bank, you wait silently in a quiet, orderly line for your brief moment face to face with the keeper of the cash. The higher you go up the chain of money, the more formal its emissaries appear, from the humble teller to the notary, accountant, stockbroker, financial planner, estate lawyer, and so on to the investment bankers dubbed by Tom Wolfe, in *The Bonfire of the Vanities,* the "Masters of the Universe."[22]

Weiss argues that the sign of excrement is threatening to cultural formations in two ways: because it "signifies a pure, wasteful expenditure, circumventing societal modes and organizations of production," and because it is "a sign of self-production, an autonomous, sovereign productivity" that springs from the individual body rather than the communal law.[23] Banks and their votaries are society's psychic defenses, shrines to the denial of the body and to the cultural order threatened by its lawless and autonomous bowels. They enforce what philosopher Slavoj Žižek calls "the mad-obscene law" that "derails the psychic equilibrium" by ordering a painful, impossible enjoyment beyond the pleasure principle.[24] Their most intimidating emblem is the mad-obscene quantity of treasure that they jealously guard in all our names, at once symbolizing and staving off the excremental anarchy that feeds the reveries and nightmares of our hidden, unacknowledged selves.

The potlatch of modernity

A capitalist economy is sustained by a limitless consumption of goods, services, materials, and machines that often have little or no clear relationship to utility or need. A daunting proportion of such economies' resources is dedicated to the production and marketing of commodities that are, in the wry phraseology of Percival and Paul Goodman, not, perhaps, absolutely necessary. Transactions involving obscene quantities of money are vital to these economies because of the wealth they put into circulation. When markets are flourishing, no one questions these excesses—they seem a natural part of things, a kind of private flatulence that doesn't smell bad to the one who produces it. But as market economics reach their peak effectiveness, the flood of gargantuan transactions can start to seem obscene, disgusting, as if the flatulence is suddenly coming from someone else. Consumption for the sake of consumption, and market strategies aimed exclusively at fueling that consumption, take on a sinful and polluted air, at least for those not directly profiting from the excessiveness. Furors are kicked up over CEO salaries, golden parachutes, and termination packages that exceed the gross domestic product of many small nations. Prices may even fall. But in economies driven by such intemperance, the invariable result is another fresh start to the same old cycle. Money and its magic continue to reign, and the stench of obscenity still wafts over the land, assaulting our bodies, minds, and spirits even as we spasmodically pretend the shit doesn't stink. Canetti again:

> Excrement . . . is loaded with our whole blood guilt. By it we know what we have murdered. It is the compressed sum of all the evidence against us. It is our daily and continuing sin and, as such, it stinks and cries to heaven. It is remarkable how we isolate ourselves with it; in special rooms, set aside for the purpose, we get rid of it; our most private moment is when we withdraw there; we are alone only with our excrement. It is clear that we are ashamed of it. It is the age-old seal of that power-process of digestion, which is enacted in darkness and which, without this, would remain hidden forever.[25]

We conclude that excessive consumption is the potlatch of modernity. It is our ritual destruction of goods, and the super-rich are our cultural scapegoats; we mock their misery and refuse to believe in their pain. Yet we feel deep down that they're suffering for our sake, consecrating their lives to the production, distribution, and marketing of things we don't really need but cannot live without. More precisely, we *can* live without them—without soft drinks, say, or flat-screen TVs, or gas-guzzling cars—but we're afraid to try, partly from habit (the marketer's best friend) and partly from a fear that the end of *consumer culture* would be the end of *culture itself,* at least in the forms we know and love.

So we keep consuming what we want rather than what we need; we keep enriching tycoons, moguls, and CEOs who are already richer than we could dream of being; we keep worshiping the dead presidents in our wallets. And all the while we detect the growing stench of lucre that's filthy, rich who are stinking, wealth that's ineffably but unmistakably obscene. When money becomes *de trop,* in Sartre's existential sense, its all-powerful excess can no longer be flushed, purged, vomited, or wiped away. It is the transhistorical human stain. Vespasian was wrong. *Pecunia olet.*

Notes

1. Robert Penn Warren, *All the King's Men* (New York: Bantam Books, 1959), 359.

2. James Strachey, *The Standard Edition of the Complete Psychological Works of Sigmund Freud,* 1959, vol. 9 (London: Vintage, 2001), 74.

3. Ibid., vol. 12, 187.

4. Ibid., vol. 17, 82–84.

5. Georges Bataille, "The Notion of Expenditure," in *Visions of Excess: Selected Writings, 1927–1939,* trans. Allan Stoekl (Minneapolis: University of Minnesota Press, 1985), 122.

6. Sandor Ferenczi, *Sex in Psycho-Analysis: Contributions to Psycho-Analysis,* trans. Ernest Jones (Boston: The Gorham Press, 1916), 321.

7. Mary Douglas, *Purity and Danger: An Analysis of Concepts of Pollution and Taboo* (London: Routledge Classics, 2002), 2.

8. Jean-Paul Sartre, *Being and Nothingness: A Phenomenological Essay on Ontology,* trans. Hazel E. Barnes (New York: Washington Square Press, 1992), 520–21.

9. Ferenczi, 275.

10. Alan Dundes, "Wet and Dry, the Evil Eye: An Essay in Indo-European and Semitic Worldview," in *The Evil Eye: A Folklore Casebook,* 257–98 (New York: Garland Publishing, 1981), 290–91.

11. Allen S. Weiss, *The Aesthetics of Excess* (Albany: State University of New York Press, 1989), 164–65.

12. Elias Canetti, *Crowds and Power,* trans. Carol Stewart (New York: Farrar, Straus and Giroux, 1984), 210.

13. Strachey, vol. 17, 84.

14. Anton Chekhov, *The Essential Tales of Chekhov,* trans. Constance Garnett (New York: Harper Perennial, 2000), 273.

15. Peter A. Olsson, "Complexities in the Psychology and Psychotherapy of the Phenomenally Wealthy," in *The Last Taboo; Money as Symbol and Reality in Psychotherapy and Psychoanalysis,* ed. David W. Krueger, 55–69 (New York: Brunner/Mazel, 1986), 61–62.

16. Dennis T Jaffe, "The Burdens of Wealth," in *Families in Business* (June 2003): 76–77. 28 [Article on-line] (accessed November 2007) Available at http://www.dennisjaffe.com/articles/BurdensofWealth.pdf; Internet, 76.

17. Peter J. Boyer, "The Deliverer," *The New Yorker,* 19 February 2007, 88.

18. Ernest Becker, *Escape from Evil* (New York, The Free Press, 1975), 65.

19. Ibid., 78.

20. Norman O. Brown, *Life Against Death: The Psychoanalytical Meaning of History,* 2nd ed. (Middletown, CT: Wesleyan University Press, 1985), 286.

21. Becker, 65.

22. Tom Wolfe, *The Bonfire of the Vanities* (New York: Bantam Books, 2001), 59.

23. Allen S. Weiss, *The Aesthetics of Excess* (Albany: State University of New York Press, 1989), 165.

24. Slavoj Žižek, *Enjoy Your Symptom! Jacques Lacan in Hollywood and out* (New York: Routledge, 1992), 182.

25. Canetti, 211.

Preludes to a Theory of Obscenity

I.

In pondering pornography one navigates between the political imperative of free expression and the moral hazard of degradation. The default positions in the debate are predictable—if you are an enemy of censorship you are expected to tolerate pornography, and if you are an enemy of pornography you are expected to tolerate censorship, but neither one does full justice to the options. There is a position that would favor both censorship and pornography: this might be something like Orwell's *1984,* where the pornography is mostly violent, or the ideology of the proto-Nazi soldiers of the 1920s Freikorps analyzed so terrifyingly in Klaus Theweleit's *Male Fantasies,* where the pornography is both sexual and violent.[1] Censorship and pornography can both serve as means of repressive mobilization—the first by denial and the second by intoxication—in militarized or fascist regimes. One could also oppose both censorship and pornography. This is the position I will explore. We are too hasty to judge, the state is too clumsy, the fact of human plurality is too deep, and the insult to democratic equality is too noxious to have censors. On the other hand, sex is too important, the imagination is too fertile a soil, the wonders of embodiment are too great, and loyalty and love are gifts too rare to let our eyes and hearts go wandering off after pictures (and other media) of disembedded eros.[2]

II.

Pornography is not the same as obscenity. Obscenity is built into the human condition. "All humans are mortal" is a statement so basic that it has always served as the first premise of a valid syllogism. As so often in philosophy, the statement marries two modes that otherwise resist each other's company: the logical and the existential. Since when were we reasonable about mortality? Why is something so basic to our existence so baffling? Contrary to popular opinion, the more elementary a concept is the harder it is to grasp. It is probably easier for a mathematician to define a "p-adic group" than a number. Biologists can tell you all about the Krebs cycle, but "life" itself, the center of their discipline, remains forever imprecise. Poets can tell a trochee from a spondee, but not what poetry is. Precision prevails in advanced studies, not basic ones. The fact that we are mortal animals may be our most difficult study.

The intellectual climate around this fact seems perpetually foggy. For philosophical edification, we need to remember that we are mortal; for everyday functioning, we need to be able to forget it. Humankind cannot bear very much reality. We are irreparably touchy about birth, copulation, and death. Our bodies are gorgeous and icky, sacred and profane at the same time. Nudity, sex, and excretion are utterly ordinary but can seem perfectly scandalous. Obscenity, the transgressive interruption of the flesh into our midst, is always at least potentially a salutary call to conscience. Whatever else it is, obscenity is offensive, and sometimes offenses must come. Pornography, on the other hand, is the coordinated production and dissemination of sexually explicit media, especially word or picture, for the sake of arousal and profit. All cultures have obscenity, but not all have pornography. Obscenity comes from bodily givens; pornography from media choices.

Friends of free expression sometimes imagine an offense-free realm in which nobody would any longer be offended by obscenity and four-letter words could pal around with their respectable synonyms. They exhort people to grow up and face facts, as if the capacity for shocked perplexity about generation and corruption could once and for all be overcome. This is the utopia of liberal free-speech theory, and it would be fit only for angels. "To the pure all things are pure" is a Pauline dictum that defenders of free sexual expression are wont to quote, but humans do not manage purity very well—the part of Paul's teaching that liberals are wont to ignore. (They also typically ignore his idea that voluntary modulation of our liberty can be a way of loving one's neighbor.) No mortal is beyond offense. Everyone will find something obscene—depictions of bodies, images of torture and abuse, a burning cross, the faces of malicious men or the size of military budgets. Offense is built into the human estate. To be alive and embodied is to be offendable. It is not something we will ever grow out of. We would lose something dear if offense were no longer a capacity. Our mortal embodiment means that obscenity will be a perennial nettle to grasp.

III.

Liberalism provides indispensable arguments for freedom, but it tends to stack the rhetorical deck against a thoughtful analysis of the bounds of carnal representation. Its anti-censorship discourse and the more general sense that limiting pornography is the same as putting women back on the pedestal and gays and lesbians back in the closet give pause. Pornography for some theorists stands in, part for whole, for emancipation.[3] Questioning porn can feel like questioning freedom.

Some of the rhetorical complexities can be seen in two contrasting books on obscenity in the United States. Marjorie Heins's *Not in Front of the Children* (2001) tells a story of unfolding openness and honesty about sexuality that leaves behind a long train of unfounded alarms about interracial marriage, sex education, birth control, etc. She shows how elastic the domain of erotic panic is and how topics now considered worthy of public discussion were once stigmatized as dangerous and indecent. Heins has a deadpan gift for assembling a rogue's gallery of tremulous quiverers before sexual threats. She makes it hard to imagine any other story than her own. The reader sits at the end of a long process of clarification and growing yet precarious reasonableness. Doubt her vindication of the pioneers of openness and you risk denying several incontestable achievements. Few people today think that we should not discuss breast cancer, AIDS, or teenage sexuality, or keep *Ulysses* or *Lady Chatterley's Lover* off the shelves. Her point is that the wheat of public enlightenment and the tares of explicit expression grow together. Pull up the tares, and you risk uprooting the wheat as well. Sex has no catastrophic moral, aesthetic, or spiritual meaning for Heins: it is a manageable topic of public debate.

Rochelle Gurstein's *The Repeal of Reticence* (1996) covers much of the same ground as Heins but from a very different point of view. Rather than emancipation we have loss. Her plaint is our growing inability to "speak the old poetic languages of love, for now they sound evasive, sentimental, platitudinous or naïve." The cult of frankness makes impossible a common world in which delicate discriminations about matters of public taste would make sense.[4] Gurstein has more of an uphill fight than Heins (even though children are often the sticking point in censorship debates). Gurstein knows full well that the direction of modern culture works against her, that the genie can't be put back in the bottle, and that calls for reticence risk being mocked as head-in-the-sand phobia. Nonetheless she gamely tries to paint modernity as the tearing away of the veil from something sacred, the violation of a mystery. In contrast to a liberal politics of clashing opinion and uninhibited debate, she roughly follows Hannah Arendt's politics of agonistic aesthetic performance in which some realms necessarily remain in obscurity—sex, life, labor, the household. The Heideggerian principle that truth shines forth most truly when it is most concealed has always been a hard sell in liberal climes, which tend to view concealment as cover-up.

Though liberal vindication has easier rhetorical work than conservative hesitation, the confrontation between what both Gurstein and Heins call "the party of exposure" and "the party of reticence" is not an easy thing to sort out. Which maxim should we follow—"Sunlight is the best disinfectant" or "all sunshine makes a desert?" Which do we want, Enlightenment or Romance, the wisdom of experience or the bloom of innocence? Which is worse, a stifled idea or a world in which nothing is sacred? It is a real conflict of values. The problems of conservative reticence are obvious—nostalgia, impracticality, and potential oppression. But liberal glasnost has problems as well—moral and metaphysical shallowness. No one seriously denies that representations of human things deserve the greatest care, but liberal thought has developed few resources to guide a policy of caution. Its absolute ban on censorship can be a political bull in an ethical china shop. We should take unrestricted free expression as one competing—and precious—value among many others, but not as an absolute. Insisting on one virtue at the expense of other virtues is sophomoric. The tragic fact, as the great Isaiah Berlin taught, and whose liberalism was unusually full of salutary murk and depth, is that many goods and values compete for attention and allegiance, and defy any final reconciliation. It is because all values never fully harmonize that we need free speech. But we should not think that free speech is a meta-value above all others; it is battling with all the rest.

IV.

What liberalism does understand well is that offense cannot provide the basis for a reasonable ethics. In time, offense looks ridiculous and reactionary. Later generations are puzzled by what all the fuss was about. Were Elvis's hips really so suggestive? (Yes.) Once an idea, text, or work of art has become public, no one can stuff it back into the private sphere. *Les jeux sont faits*. It becomes part of the common world, something we can't imagine ever having not existed. That offense is not an ethically sustainable program arms the liberal historian like Heins with a ready-made triumphal narrative.

A compelling version of the liberal attack against offense has been given by Martha Nussbaum. Her criticism of disgust and qualified defense of anger provides a vision of the liberal emotional order. Anger, she argues, would be impossible without a sense of justice. It is tied to our sense of right and wrong. Indignation for her can change the world in a way that disgust never can. A world without outrage would be deprived of justice (or else would have to be an improbable utopia in which we would have no reason ever to be angry). It is a gamble, of course, to hitch the liberal wagon to anger, as she well knows. The wrath of Achilles made an awful mess out of things. But at least anger has a potentially rational core; it could meet the Kantian maxim of generalizability in the sense that there are some things that you could wish everyone would be angry about (the abuse of children, for instance). Disgust, in contrast, she finds suspicious as an ethical-political guide for several reasons: its cognitive content is unreliable, it involves magical thinking, and it is a denial of the fluid basis of our common mortality. With disgust we hide from humanity (in the sense of mortal embodiment); with anger we potentially fight for it (in the sense of ethical solidarity). More importantly, disgust usually involves veiled social distinctions and hierarchies. Disgusts about food, smell, or bodily fluids are often visceral renderings of anxieties about people who are different from us. Used as a basis of social and legal policy, disgust risks enshrining forms of oppression and abuse. Disgust cannot withstand the Kantian test of universalizability: we cannot wish that everyone would be disgusted by, say, homosexuality or the eating of pork without excluding some portion of the human species. Disgust defies an ultimate rational filter.[5]

In claiming the moral superiority of outrage Nussbaum lets another emotion in through the back door—pride, the Achilles' heel of liberalism.

Consider the social psychology of self-justification. "Attribution error" is the tendency to interpret our own behavior as motivated by reason and circumstance and other people's behavior as motivated by disposition and will. Since we know our own minds better than those of others, we tend to cut ourselves a certain explanatory slack. If I cut someone off in traffic, it is because I am late to work or upset about a sick child; if someone cuts me off, it is because they are rude or incon-siderate. I perceive my own behavior as governed by the fluidity of con-text and that of other people as governed by the rigidity of character. We interpret our own conduct situationally and other people's conduct dispositionally. I was late; he is a jerk.[6]

This analysis of the way we provide ourselves ethical discounts illu-minates the dynamics of offense. Offenders rarely think themselves offenders. Offense is more often taken than given. It is more generally a matter of reception than intention, more often attributed than perpe-trated. This means that when Peter takes offense from Paul, Peter may feel justified in giving it back. Paul, not recognizing that he offended Peter, is now in precisely the same position as Peter just was: respond-ing to an unprovoked assault. An offense is almost always a felt response to another's offense. Since offenders think they are only acting in self-defense, a vicious cycle of retaliation can start. Violence is usually a strike against the violence of the other.[7] Few people admit to unmoti-vated aggression. Motives for self-defense are as psychologically plen-tiful as huckleberries. As anyone who has ever broken up a squabble among children knows, no one ever started a conflict: it was always the other. Those who fight violence often do violence themselves.

V.

There is both an ethics and an epistemology here that feeds liberal thought richly. The ethics is that recognition of our own fallibility should motivate us to respond to offenses by self-critically examining our premises and seeking to understand the thought we hate. The epis-temology is similar: that our cognitive self-surety blinds us to learning opportunities. Instead of getting mad at ideas we find infuriating, we should undergo the education of learning to think with the enemy. Free speech is thus designed to humble the ego's claim to think itself always right.

Liberalism often fails to extend this analysis to its own analysis. It does not imagine that anyone could reasonably entertain a vision of the public sphere that is not of agonistic debate or a vision of the self that does not take joy in self-criticism. So it ends up creating a zone of immunity for itself in which it denies any other worldview. Thus Flem-ming Rose, the Danish newspaper editor, was offended by what he saw as a chilling effect exerted by Islam on public expression, so he com-missioned and published cartoons depicting the prophet Mohammad in response. He thought he was righting an offense against free speech. Though no one could have envisioned the chain of escalating cause and effect that led to riots, boycotts, and killings around the world, Rose saw himself as standing up to a bully. He did not consider himself an aggressor; he was giving as good as he got. Censorship, as every liberal knows, is a form of class privilege (claiming a right for the censor that is denied to others, that of access to materials). But denouncing censorship is also a form of class privilege. (To advocate free speech is often an offensive act.) The chorus celebrating free expression during the cartoon controversy by some but not all Europeans and North Americans was more than a hymn to liberty: it was a bid for civilizational supremacy. Free expression symbolically separated enlightened Europe from benighted Islam.[8]

There can be a kind of imperial privilege and luxury in advertising the fortitude of one's toleration or the intensity of one's commitment to liberty. Opposing censorship is not a simple virtuous act; it is a seizure of the prime ethical real estate in the public sphere. There is a theatrical side to denouncing censorship. Liberals like to think of themselves as the neutral arbiters of public debate, but they are adherents to a "fighting creed," as Charles Taylor says.[9] Their questioning of all monopolies rarely extends to their monopoly right to manage the public sphere. Campaigns against censorship can be a kind of moral bullying (*crusades* might be the correct term in the Danish case).[10]

One lesson from the Danish cartoon controversy is that taking offense about the other's offense is a form of engagement, not a neutral spectatorial act. Rose's way of being offended offended others. Offense is not the same as disgust, of course, but absolutist free-speech advocates are too quick to see taking offense as something that only the others do. Liberals dislike the low-rent offense of disgust and prefer its high-rent sibling, indignation. The art of taking offense can be a luxurious repertoire of moral gestures that is just as available to the liberally educated as to the unlettered. In taking offense we can accuse, show off our delicacy, and shame the coarse for their brutishness or the lukewarm for their insufficient zeal. Indignation can be a kind of blackmail: sign the petition or be complicit with evil.

Moreover, few things are quite as delicious as the feeling of being offended. Though her tone is more even-handed than some of her colleagues in the ACLU, Heins engages in a common rhetorical strategy of ticking off outrages against free speech in order to gather righteousness for her side. Taking offense is contagious; it is always tempting to jump on the bandwagon of indignation. By being scandalized by obscenity

I show that I am not a pervert; by being scandalized by people scandalized by obscenity, I show that I am not a prude. Not only does it feel good to be offended; it can also look good. Indignation is one of the most manipulable of emotions—perhaps because it plays less to our appetites than to our sense of ourselves as righteous and reasonable. We can cherish our grudges like household pets; the same with our indignations. Being wronged suggests we are right. Being a victim can supply a purity and innocence. (The moral of the history of American military intervention might be: beware of outraged innocents, especially if they have big guns.[11]) The liberal offense at people who are offended by obscenity can be a form of class warfare. Both sides consider themselves innocent—a failsafe recipe for escalating conflict. What Pascal and Rousseau called *amour-propre* can cause as much mischief as disgust or lust.

Indignation may be a virtue in some contexts, but free-speech advocacy has few checks against the tendency to invidious self-justification. Nussbaum's limited endorsement of anger does nothing to discourage the moral tyranny of a righteous cause. Liberal outrage about the outrage of the other is its own form of outrage. Liberalism's claim to occupy the high ground can unwittingly undermine its epistemology of fallibility and ethic of maximizing learning opportunities.

VI.

Take a lesson from Marx. Who, he asked in one of his moments of black humor, is the most productive worker in capitalism? The criminal, of course. Not only do criminals exemplify the basic modus operandi of the system, that of unlawful acquisition, but they also sustain a web of other workers such as professors of criminal law, constables, judges, and hangmen; they give rise to art, novels, and plays; and they keep bourgeois society refreshed from its monotony.[12] I am not aware that any Marxist scholar has exploited this fruitful insight for the culture industries in general.[13] As a media genre, scandal has been the lifeblood of the popular press since the early nineteenth century. The history of modern art, cinema, literature, and music is a history of enormously productive scandals, from Stravinsky's *Rite of Spring* to Damien Hirst's plasticized sheep. Many an artistic career has been made on *succès de scandale,* and liberal defenses of free expression depend on the transgressive vitality of deviant figures to stir things up: "abyss-artists," as I call them.[14] But scandal is a highly conservative genre. It does not criticize social norms: in exposing people for violating them it presupposes and thereby *reinforces* them.[15] Marx's point was that the criminal *sustains* bourgeois order.

Liberalism loves tropes of illumination, but it tends to see light as exposure and not as transformation. Its modus operandi of exposing the hidden is structurally identical with obscenity. Liberalism, as a boundary-buster of public and private, is obscene. The public sphere has something to do with the pubic sphere, as the typos of my students regularly have it. Of course we can be grateful to the journalism of outrage for exposing institutional wrongdoing, and more generally to the acids of enlightenment for unmasking illusions.[16] But it is itself obscene—in the sense of an offense against human solidarity—to see our carnal ordinariness as scandalous. Failure to distinguish political from ethical exposé fuels the pornographic itch. To publicize is to put into circulation, and the light of the public gaze changes the nature of some things. As Arendt said: "The heart knows . . . that what was straight when it was hidden must appear crooked when it is displayed."[17] However noble your motives might feel inside, once you explain them they become self-serving. The simple fact of staging them before others corrupts them. The public is the realm of third parties, and everyone knows that being watched or overheard can change everything. No soul can be entirely "out." No mind or heart could bear full publication. The menu of media scandal consists of ordinary vices magnified by publicity: vanity, pettiness, lust, gluttony, or hypocrisy. Many dreams and desires are made tawdry by being uttered. Inside, they are fond and silly wishes; in public they are porn and crime. Publication can make human ordinariness monstrous. (The promise of the reality TV genre is to make ordinary people just as scandalous as celebrities.) The fog of privacy keeps us lovable. The attraction and moral deficit of scandal reporting is its flattery that we are only spectators and not participants in the fascinating flaws it uncovers.

Scandal and liberalism share the angelic position: the delusion that we could be exempt from the claims of the flesh. There is a contagion of prurience even in the most academic or legalistic discussions of free sexual expression. Any word with a potential double entendre will quickly embrace it; inadvertent puns sprout like toadstools. There is no safe metalanguage for discussing obscenity. Quotation marks, as a purification ritual, only displace the fact that you are still choosing to use the words. Description is already participation. The upright Ken Starr, the U.S. Solicitor General who wrote the report on the Clinton–Lewinsky affair, thought himself an investigator, but he also was an inadvertent pornographer.[18] He was certainly no liberal politically, but he banked on the notion that the analyst could eke out some kind of immunity. Lenny Bruce sardonically noted how zealously the judge and prosecutor repeated the ten-letter word that they were trying him for having uttered in public.[19] There is no exemption from human things. The censor is exactly the same type of creature as the transgressor, a sexual fleshy being prone to obscenity. Mercy is a better response to revelation than scandal.

Scandal involves the revelation of what we always knew anyway. It is an ever-renewable fountain. All of us are just one "wardrobe malfunction" away from indecent exposure. Obscenity is a perpetually available human resource. In the temple, things are sacred; outside the very same things are profane (from the Latin *pro fanum*, in front of the temple). Obscenity consists in desecrated boundaries; the barrier between purity and danger is sometimes a see-through garment. Sexologist Havelock Ellis seems to have afflicted us with the ineradicable notion that *obscene* means off-the-scene or off stage, *scaena* (stage) being his supposed Latin root.[20] Justice Warren Burger traced *obscene* to the Latin *caenum* (filth).[21] The evidence for either etymology is thin. Indeed, the historical attestation of the word is as obscure as the attestation of the thing. The history of the word is vague and messy because evasion might be obscenity's defining mark as much as any particular content. The subtitle to Ludwig Marcuse's fine book on obscenity could well be translated as "the history of an exasperation."

Obscenity is one of the oldest things around, and yet it always manages to feel fresh. Marcuse quotes a definition of obscenity from 1688 that in some ways seems just as relevant today: "clearly lewd discourses [that] speak impudently of sex organs or paint the acts of debauched and impure people in such a way that chaste and tender ears shrink from them in fright."[22] The summits of lascivious depiction were surely reached millennia ago. And yet obscenity always seems to push the latest envelope of taboo. What, ask the shocked by-standers, will they think of next? Like the second law of thermodynamics, modernity seems to run in only one direction: ever-increasing degradation. One study of trends in risqué TV advertising was headlined, "By 2046 they will all be naked." Of course that omega-point will never be reached, since covering and its modulation maintain the perennial allure of the body. Both culture industries and the avant-garde promote a rhetoric of the next step, although both are fashion systems based more on recycling than conquering frontiers. Obscenity is evergreen.

The truly liberal response might be not only never to be shocked by obscenity, but also never to be shocked by the endless ability of obscenity to shock. We all have bodies. They produce splendid ooze. Covering them is as important as uncovering them. They will always be unmanageably uncanny. Only the gods would know nothing obscene.

VII.

Humans are creatures who live both in the light of day and in the shadow of night. Exposure can undeniably be a path to progressive social reform, but there is a dialectic of enlightenment to be considered. I allude, of course, to one of the great and strange books of the twentieth century, *Dialektik der Aufklärung,* a series of philosophical-historical fragments dictated by the German-Jewish philosophers Max Horkheimer and Theodor Adorno in their Santa Monica "exile" in 1944. In contrast to liberal thought, they do not take Enlightenment as an unalloyed good thing. We moderns pay for our reasonableness with an inner hardening, a routinization of suffering in the self that justifies administering it to others, and a diffuse stoicism that impedes connection with otherness, intoxication or even faith. Reason disenchants the world, saving us from demons and charlatans, but disenchantment has violent side effects, demonizing those others (such as women, Jews, and animals) who lack a berth on the *S.S. Enlightenment.* Odysseus is Horkheimer and Adorno's—rather preposterous— image of the bourgeois subject, tied to the mast of the ship listening to the sirens sing while the slave rowers grunt below. Odysseus neuters the sirens' song of all that is begotten, born, or dies. His resourceful sublimation gives him power over the prehistoric world of sound and women, over the slaves, and over himself. Ascetic reason frees the bourgeoisie from the bonds of myth but steers it into the doldrums of disillusionment. And enlightenment does its most ambiguous work in the sexual domain, reducing fond or foolish reverie into physical acts and organs. Sade, as they note, is the zenith of sexual enlightenment.[23] Like most high modernists, Horkheimer and Adorno adored sex and despised pornography—quite as they adored Beethoven and the burlesque, and hated jazz and Hollywood. Sublimation was great and so was desublimation, but the perpetual sugar tease of mass culture was sickening.

They floated the idea of a *Bilderverbot,* or ban on images.[24] This notion, which stems from the second of the ten Mosaic commandments and finds iconoclastic strains in Judaism, Christianity, and Islam, became important later in critical theory as a way to ponder the limits of representation in depicting the Shoah or Holocaust. The obscene thing would be trying to represent what happened at Auschwitz at all. Obviously, such cautions are not forms of censorship or suppression, but are sensitive to the formal metamorphosis, transfiguration or even redemption that artistic rendering can impose.[25] Publication can change ontology. Form matters. The specificities of mediation and communication are not mere packing material. A rhetoric of reticence builds a "zone of silence" around the mystery of personhood—the same mystery that Nazism violated.[26] Explicitness can impoverish. Michel Foucault's *Discipline and Punish* is an update of *Dialectic of Enlightenment* in this respect: both books anatomize liberal humanism, ask how oppressive the gaze can be, and cast doubts on the policy of always leaving the lights on. "Visibility is a trap," in Foucault's famous but rarely heeded words. A decent respect to the opinions of mankind might let us extend the courtesy of circumspection to sex as well as violence. Foucault found nothing liberating in the modern obsessive chattiness about sex. Mushrooms grow in the dark. Voluptuaries have as much to fear from pornography as do prudes.[27]

VIII.

The theory of free expression was born twins with the printing press. Literate adults were the assumed audience for the public sphere—Mill in *On Liberty* excluded children and "barbarians" from public debate without batting an eye. What is liberalism supposed to do with images, sounds, and the Internet? How is the philosophy of free expression to respond to the waning of critical literacy as the normative cognitive mode for citizens? The question, to be sure, is not completely one of media forms per se. A world of digital pictures and sounds is not inherently any wilder than one of gossip, song, and print. Eighteenth-century Paris, as we know from Robert Darnton, had a vibrant and often scurrilous multi-media system in which rumor and gossip, especially about the royal court, circulated by word-of-mouth rumor, song and manuscript, pamphlets and books. Indeed, Enlightenment Paris is one birthplace of modern pornography, which was at first a genre of aristocratic intrigues and political critique.[28] The twenty-first century has no monopoly on communication out of control.

And yet an analysis of the materialities of communication should inform any responsible theory of free speech. The mainstreaming of pornography is one of the great stories of our time. Its recent rise to centrality in popular culture is a result of both technical transformations and societal decisions. From the eighteenth century through the later twentieth century, modern pornography was largely a literary matter, though there have always been pictures. Literacy was a chief barrier to access, and channels of distribution were largely underground. Today the ecology of communication in general has shifted with significant implications for porn. In the U.S. in the 1960s, you were lucky to view four channels on your TV screen full of least-common-denominator programming; today on an appropriately linked computer screen, you can watch almost whatever niche fare you want. Inhibitions that once ruled both production and consumption have waned. The diffusion of new platforms for content delivery such as mobile phones and computers makes media choices more and more a matter of private discretion. YouTube's slogan "broadcast yourself" nicely captures the reorganization of the past decades. Broadcasting was once mass, collective, and impersonal: today it is a medium of individual self-expression. In some sense, pornography is the "truth" of the middle-class communication situation today: it is privately viewed, digital, networked, virtual in sociability, and based as much in image as text. Anthony Giddens calls modernity a process of disembedding, and pornography today is partly a double disembedding, both of communication (from social monitoring) and of sex (from presence).

A few keystrokes can conjure sexually explicit content with historically unprecedented speed and indiscriminateness. Pornography has moved out of specialty shops, the mails, and clandestinely circulated publications into the home and office. It has jumped from print to pixels. It shapes the fashions people wear and the deeds people do, and it perhaps has its subtlest effect on the vital but immeasurable realm of the collective imagination. To reify something that is as essential and as mysterious to our humanity as sexuality into publicly accessible matter without regard to the context or covenant of its expression seems to me a potential form of civilizational suicide. What does it mean to fall in love with pictures? Sex is already our medium of existence, but pornography distills it into an uninhabitable perfume. Media always imply storage and transmission: what does it mean to bottle up sex for decontextualized use? The rise of porn as a multi-billion-dollar industry should be a huge challenge to the classic liberal confidence that anything goes.[29] In radically changed conditions of communication and shifting cultural norms, we might have better targets than Victorian prudery.

IX.

The disembodiment of sex by audiovisual media is as potentially significant to human history as the disembodiment of mind by writing. Plato's *Phaedrus* stages the age-old fears that new media both disembody our souls and set loose new kinds of sexual predators. (These are intimately related.) That the writer can reach out from the text and take possession of the reader's voice—which reads aloud—symbolizes the erotic capture of the body at a distance.[30] In the same way, MySpace and Facebook are eager to show their propriety in taking measures against sexual predators. Every new medium harbors (fantasies of) such creatures.

Media—devices that arrange souls and bodies in space and time— always have erotic implications. Every media extension of the body, according to one of Marshall McLuhan's best ideas, is also an amputation. Despite his posthumous christening by *Wired* magazine as the prophet of cyberspace, McLuhan was no fan of virtual disembodiment. Though he was not very consistent on this count (or any other), he often scorned the dream of electronic transcendence as "angelism." Pornography can be understood precisely in his sense as an amputating extension. It is the zenith of a trend he noted, the absorption of touch and the other senses into the hypertrophy of the eye. It trades haptics for optics. Pornography is the most physiological of all media (most of which have physiological implications). The user (note the druggie language) is exalted into solipsistic grandeur. Porn, like liberalism, holds out the dream of free individualistic consumer choice, and even more, of not being bound by the finitude of the flesh.

Porn amps the gap between desire and sex. Said Aldous Huxley: "Many people are more agreeably excited by the representation— whether pictorial or verbal—than by the carnal reality. It is a curious psychological fact, for which I can find no complete explanation."[31] The imagination can go places the body cannot. Lust, as Augustine said, does not drive us into the flesh: it exposes the painful gap between flesh and spirit. D. H. Lawrence, who complained that pornography made sex mental instead of bodily, might have been surprised to find himself scooped by the church father, but they agreed about the dangerous ways that lustful imagination side-stepped the blessings of being a mortal creature. Desire, said Thomas Hobbes, is the absence of the object; love is its presence. (Here he followed Plato's *Symposium*). "In pleasure," said Goethe's Faust, "I thirst for desire."[32] Desire is already obstreperous enough, but porn distends the ratio between desire and sex. We have "minds that can wander beyond all limit and satiety."[33] Desire is potentially infinite, but sex, even at its most athletic, is always finite. The joint activity of friendly bodies making love need not have a lot to do with the pulsating imagination, although fiction does seem part of everything humans do.

Porn's dishonor of presence has something to do with the photographic medium and its code of realism. Like all realism it is dishonest in its suppression of the mediating artifice. Music—perhaps the greatest erotic medium—handles desire differently. (As the old saying goes, there is an orgasm in Tchaikovsky every seven minutes.[34]) Music is both the most abstract and the most emotive of all arts. Music brings forth feeling in sound and time, but it is immune to fetishism in a way that pictures never can be. The eroticism of music is generally abstract; that of pornography is concrete. Music presents a utopia of generality, a way of being in an unspecified body. Music escapes positivity; photography captures contingency.

Pornography is in league with a historical and social process of abstracting sexuality from spiritual, social, and emotional anchorage. It comes in a line of descent from materialist thought in seventeenth- and eighteenth-century Europe. The bodies in motion of enlightenment philosophy, as Margaret Jacob shows, mirrored the newly atomized sociability of urban life and of the new genre of the pornographic novel.[35] On the question whether sexuality is a zone of free play or is embedded in larger narratives and practices, pornography clearly votes for differentiation—of sex from other realms and of organs from the body.[36] Pornography's treatment of sex as plastic pleasures removed from duties and persons fits the modern division of labor. It also fits the trend in modern media of transporting distant bodies as sights, sounds, and words. Interaction with distant people as symbolic effigies is one of the major transformations of modern times.[37] Touch is no guarantee of ease or quality in linguistic or nonverbal interaction—but it is essential in sexual interaction. Porn provides sex without touch or the other. It does away with the object. The objectification of the person in the picture is paired to the subjectification of the viewer. The emancipation of sexual desire from the mortal, imperfect beloved is one of porn's chief deficits. Too much perfection makes us sick.

X.

Liberals rarely admit (though they know very well) that pornography is not just a consumer choice but a battlefield for spiritual authority, a contest about what institutions and practices get to preside over inner life and its irrigation. ACLU head Nadine Strossen, for instance, pairs her defense of pornography with a superficial picture of the sexual person. She marshals much useful evidence to show how legislative attempts to control porn backfire, but she does not see sexuality as open to degradation—or chastity as a positive good. Without even the usual invocation of social science research on minimal media effects, she can imagine no harm in sex or pornography: it is all happy consensual healthy fun. Though her antagonist Catherine MacKinnon's vision of sexuality is dire and bleak, rape and heterosexual intercourse being indistinguishable, MacKinnon at least grasps what one might call the Baudelairean side of sex. At one point Strossen dismisses Augustine together with Puritans, Victorians, Christian fundamentalists, and anti-pornography feminists in one fell swoop.[38] No doubt, some things Augustine said left a lasting blot, but his sense for the experience of mortal creatures is hauntingly resonant—the proximity of pleasure and pain, sex and violence, delight and degradation. What Nietzsche said of Paul counts better for Augustine or his legatee Freud: he is a "dysangelist," a bringer of bad tidings. We dismiss such insights at the risk of our own shallowness.

In the modern world, pornography was first a political genre, and it is partly on political grounds that I oppose it. We need the solidity of a public world against Jacobin jouissance, the eros of revolutionary violence. Lust means the suspension of social order: its lesson is the thought that society no longer exists with its contracts, commitments, and relations. Lust can create a very exciting kind of counter-order or communitas, but it is not a sustainable program.[39] Kin, lover, friend, citizen, and stranger are crucially different kinds of relations. Pornography promises to eradicate the saving distance in human contact. Immediacy is always a lie. (This is the chief link from ethics to media studies.) Representative institutions create complex webs of mediacy between people. Porn is to love what revolution is to democracy—a magnification of an essential destructive element at the core of each. "The most tender place in my heart is for strangers," sings Neko Case. It can be so much easier to fall in love with passing phantoms than to live with people for years. What checks do we have against the vertigo of bad infinity?

One should be able to both favor free expression and consider the porn industry a cultural, spiritual, ethical, and political catastrophe. Liberalism shares the ecological idea that maximization of diversity is the surest path to future viability. In wildness is the preservation of the world. But environmental analysis does not renounce judgment: it knows of blights and species that run rampant. Why is this kind of judgment so difficult for the ecologist of speech? (One reason is liberal philosophy's insufficiently examined equation of market competition and the discovery of truth.) If we want maximal diversity, we might well be appalled by the proliferation of some species. One can join the civil libertarians in their defense of free speech and still find pornography a plague in the land.

XI.

The critics of obscenity of late are often less formidable intellectually than they are politically. This is not true of the granddaddy of them all, Moses, the fiercest and deepest thinker there is on obscenity. Plato, who comes in a close second, seems to have thought that bodily begetting was inferior to intellectual begetting; the anti-sex impulse in western thought and culture is in his lineage, not Moses'. Genesis, his first book in the traditional but discredited view of biblical authorship, concerns the familial adventures of the phallus, its circumcision, covenant, and begettings. Exodus, his second, concerns the political struggle for liberation from captivity and the long journey to the Promised Land. (Genesis is the book of Freud, Exodus the book of Marx.)[40] Sexuality for Moses was bound by law. It was to be properly embedded in a covenant relationship. Ever since, we have been trying to wriggle out of the box of sex as justice. Those who think that we can call the whole thing off and start over in Edenic innocence, or look forward to the millennial day when sex operates under some other sign than law are, in my view, not fully informed. The longing for the innocence of the sexual dawn or for the lifting of the strictures of the law are well-established impulses in the Mosaic legacy. These remain the stories of the post-European world, for good and ill, and the infrastructure of its unconscious. When we think we can bypass this tradition, we only find it waiting for us at the end of the road.

Whatever, whoever, if ever Moses was, his name stands for a mix of currents and gestures: law-giving, people-formation, covenant-making, idol-smashing, and sacred writing. The deep structure of our worries about obscenity has something deep to do with monotheism. A single god is a jealous god, prone to wrath, indignation, and even disgust. The main target of biblical wrath is idols—competitor deities, often female ones full of fertility and sexuality, ever alluring with their images and devotees in their temples. Idolatry is always figured as adultery by the

Hebrew prophets, as the people of Israel breaking their marriage covenant with God. The second of the ten Mosaic commandments proclaims, as noted, a *Bilderverbot* or ban on images. A media policy against visual representations in favor of the text was a religious matter. God was aniconic, appearing by writing or sound, but never by visual image.[41] Monotheism's first target, we might say, was pornography.

The friends of liberty are sometimes tempted to dismiss the monotheistic heritage as censorious and intolerant, and to see its "fundamentalist" descendents as the major threat to free expression today—which they might be. (I'd add the market and the state.) But liberalism also owes to monotheism its central gesture of an incandescent all-seeing reason. World-historically, monotheism has blazing epistemological accomplishments. Iconoclasm (the smashing of images), said Hegel, is the precondition of analytic thinking. A transcendent god leaves worldly zones evacuated of the divine—specifically the idols themselves, which are made of mere wood and stone. Monotheism opens up the world to a liberty of human action apart from divine control—a religiously neutral space apt for scientific experimentation, interreligious toleration, and debates in the public sphere. A notion of secular empty matter is not found in more relaxed polytheistic cultures. There the gods are everywhere; so often is sexuality. Sexual discipline and intellectual achievement coincide; Freud was not original in noting the epistemocarnal doubleness of the biblical term "to know" or the fruits of sublimation.[42]

Moses' legacy is a deeply mixed bag and deserves more than this teaser (and let us be extremely careful here, for this narrative can be hijacked for anti-Semitic purposes). It provides a vocabulary of outrage and revulsion that has never been surpassed: "a stench in my nostrils," "an abomination." (Outrage about idols often meant violence against idol-worshippers.) But it also tells the story of family lineage, the Promised Land, of a peace and justice that would fill the whole earth. It founds a patriarchal order that—speaking of obscenity—ritualistically cuts the penis as a sign of the promise with God (*berit* or *bris* = circumcision and covenant). Moses gave the shelter of legal and lawful covenant to something as flammable as sex. Moses was not anti-sex: he was pro-sex and anti-idol. He wanted the one true god, not the many false ones, to preside over sex. Whether his legacy is one major part of the long reign of heteronormative patriarchy or the binding of male sexuality to fidelity and care is an open question. Odds are we won't get over our troubles about obscenity any time soon, and that might be a very fine thing.[43]

Notes

1. Klaus Theweleit, *Male Fantasies*, trans. Stephan Conway (Minneapolis: University of Minnesota Press, 1987–89), 2 vols.

2. I leave aside the very difficult but more obvious question of the damage pornography does to women and focus instead on the subtler phenomenology of damage to the (male) user, taking courage from the older volume, *Men Confront Pornography*, ed. Michael S. Kimmel (New York: Crown, 1990).

3. See, for instance, Edward DeGrazia, *Girls Lean Back Everywhere* (New York: Random House, 1992); Nadine Strossen, *Defending Pornography* (New York: Scribner, 1995); and Linda Williams, *Hard Core* (Berkeley: University of California Press, 1999).

4. Marjorie Heins, *Not in Front of the Children: "Indecency," Censorship, and the Innocence of Youth* (New York: Hill and Wang, 2001); Rochelle Gurstein, *The Repeal of Reticence: A History of America's Cultural and Legal Struggles over Free Speech, Obscenity, Sexual Liberation, and Modern Art* (New York: Hill and Wang, 1996), 7.

5. Martha C. Nussbaum, *Hiding from Humanity: Disgust, Shame, and the Law* (Princeton: Princeton University Press, 2004).

6. Fritz Heider, *The Psychology of Interpersonal Relations* (New York: Wiley, 1958), 30–35, is a key source.

7. Jean-Paul Sartre, *Critique of Dialectical Reason*, trans. Alan Sheridan-Smith (1960; London: NLB, 1982), 1:133.

8. See Elisabeth Eide, Risto Kunelius, Angela Phillips, eds., *Transnational Media Events: The Mohammed Cartoons and the Imagined Clash of Civilizations* (Göteborg: NORDICOM, 2008).

9. Charles Taylor, "The Politics of Recognition," in *Multiculturalism: Examining the Politics of Recognition*, ed. Amy Gutmann (Princeton, NJ: Princeton University Press, 1994), 62.

10. Empirical studies show that men support free-speech rights more than women, and that rich countries do so more than poor countries. Liberalism presupposes security. See Julie L. Andsager, Robert O. Wyatt, and Ernest L. Martin, *Free Expression and Five Democratic Publics* (Cresskill, NJ: Hampton Press, 2004).

11. See my "La pitié, la terreur, et l'enigme de l'assassin vertueux," *La terreur spectacle: Terrorisme et télévision*, ed. and trans. Daniel Dayan (Paris: Éditions Boeck, 2006), 247–60.

12. Karl Marx, "Apologist Conception of the Productivity of All Professions," *Theories of Surplus Value*, vol. 1 (London: Lawrence and Wishart, 1969), 387–88.

13. With the possible exception of Ernst Mandel, *Delightful Murder: A Social History of the Crime Story* (London: Pluto Press, 1984).

14. See *Courting the Abyss* (Chicago: University of Chicago Press, 2005), 86–97.

15. Paul F. Lazarsfeld and Robert K. Merton, "Mass Communication, Popular Taste, and Organized Social Action," in *The Communication of Ideas*, ed. Lyman Bryson (New York: Harper, 1948), 95–118.

16. See the unparalleled analysis of the dialectics of enlightenment in Peter Sloterdijk, *Critique of Cynical Reason*, trans. Michael Eldred (Minneapolis: University of Minnesota Press, 1987), 22–75.

17. Hannah Arendt, *On Revolution* (New York: Viking Press, 1963), 92.

18. Linda Williams, "Porn Studies: Proliferating Pornographies On/Scene: An Introduction," *Porn Studies* (Durham, NC: Duke University Press, 2004), 1–23.

19. *The Essential Lenny Bruce* (New York: Ballantine, 1967), esp. 247–48.

20. Havelock Ellis, *More Essays of Love and Virtue* (Garden City, NJ: Garden City Publishing, 1937), 100.

21. *Miller v. California* (1973), 413 U. S. 15, 18–19 (footnote 2).

22. Ludwig Marcuse, *Obszön: Geschichte einer Entrüstung* (Munich: Paul List, 1962), 20.

23. Max Horkheimer and Theodor W. Adorno, *Dialektik der Aufklärung* (Frankfurt: Fischer, 2006).

24. They do not use the exact term: "Gerettet wird das Recht des Bildes in der treuen Durchführung seines Verbots" [The right of the image is rescued in the faithful observance of its prohibition]. *Dialektik*, 30.

25. Herbert Marcuse, *The Aesthetic Dimension* (Boston: Beacon, 1978), 55–56.

26. George Steiner, *On Difficulty and Other Essays* (Oxford: Oxford University Press, 1978), 61–136. This is perhaps one reason that Nazism is such a ripe source for pornography: see Amit Pinchevski and Roy Brand, "Holocaust Perversions: The Stalags Pulp Fiction and the Eichmann Trial," *Critical Studies in Media Communication* 24.5 (2007): 387–407.

27. The classic case is D. H. Lawrence, *Pornography and Obscenity* (London: Faber and Faber, 1929).

28. Robert Darnton, "An Early Information Society: News and the Media in Eighteenth-Century Paris," *American Historical Review* 105 (2000): 1–35.

29. Jaime Nubiola, "Torturas y pornografía: la degradación de la humanidad," *Pensar en Libertad* (Pamplona: EUNSA, 2007), 119–22.

30. Jesper Svenbro, *Phrasikleia: anthropologie de la lecture en Grèce ancienne* (Paris: Découverte, 1988).

31. Aldous Huxley, *Jesting Pilate: The Diary of a Journey* (London: Chatto and Windus, 1926), 4.

32. Goethe, *Faust:* "So tauml' ich von Begierde zu Genuß, / Und im Genuß verschmacht' ich nach Begierde."

33. *Areopagitica*, in *John Milton: Complete Poems and Major Prose*, ed. Merritt Y. Hughes (New York: Odyssey Press, 1957), 733. This text, of course, has passages of astounding obscenity.

34. Michael Hicks, "The Beautiful and the Darned," *Sunstone* 54 (March 1986): 12–17.

35. Margaret C. Jacob, "The Materialist World of Pornography," *The Invention of Pornography: Obscenity and the Origins of Modernity, 1500–1800*, ed. Lynn Hunt (New York: Zone Books, 1993), 157–202.

36. Walter Kendrick, *The Secret Museum* (New York: Viking, 1987), 65.

37. See my *Speaking into the Air* (Chicago: University of Chicago Press, 1999), chapters 4–5.

38. Strossen, *Defending Pornography*, 116.

39. Roberto Mangabeira Unger, *Passion* (New York: Free Press, 1984), 174–81, 220–47.

40. Leviticus is the book of Mary Douglas.

41. For one locus classicus, see Deuteronomy chapter 4.

42. My thinking here owes much to Jean-Joseph Goux, *Les iconoclastes* (Paris: Seuil, 1978), and Geoffrey Winthrop-Young, "Memories of the Nile: Egyptian Traumas and Communication Technologies in Jan Assmann's Theory of Cultural Memory," *New German Critique* 96 (Fall 2005): 103–33. There is a longer line of reflection on Moses including Hegel, Freud, Thomas Mann, Peter Sloterdijk, and Assmann.

43. I am grateful for advice and support to Julie Andsager, Gigi Durham, Loren Glass, Samantha Joyce, Frank Kessler, Xinghua Li, Jaime Nubiola, Margaret Schwartz, Fred Turner, and an anonymous reviewer—none of whom is remotely responsible for anything in here. Audiences at the University of Iowa and London School of Economics gave helpful feedback.

Select Bibliography

Bataille, Georges. *Visions of Excess: Selected Writings, 1927–1939*. Trans. Allan Stoekl. Minneapolis: University of Minnesota Press, 1985.

Beisel, Nicola. *Imperiled Innocents: Anthony Comstock and Family Reproduction in Victorian America*. Princeton: Princeton University Press, 1997.

Boyer, Paul S. *Purity in Print: Book Censorship in America from the Gilded Age to the Computer Age*. Madison: University of Wisconsin Press, 1968.

Cornell, Drusilla, ed. *Feminism and Pornography*. New York: Oxford University Press, 2000.

DeGrazia, Edward. *Girls Lean Back Everywhere*. New York: Random House, 1992.

Dollimore, Jonathan. *Sex, Literature, and Censorship*. Cambridge: Polity, 2001.

Dore, Florence. *The Novel and the Obscene: Sexual Subjects in American Modernism*. Palo Alto, CA: Stanford University Press, 2005.

Douglas, Mary. *Purity and Danger: An Analysis of Concepts of Pollution and Taboo*. London: Routledge Classics, 2002.

Foucault, Michel. *History of Sexuality, Vol. 1: An Introduction*. Trans. Robert Hurley. New York: Vintage Books, 1978, 1990.

———. "Society Must Be Defended." *Lectures at the Collège De France 1975–1976*. Trans. David Macey. New York: Picador, 2003.

Freud, Sigmund. *The Standard Edition of the Complete Psychological Works of Sigmund Freud*. Trans. James Strachey. London: Vintage, 2001.

Friedman, Andrea. *Prurient Interests: Gender, Democracy, and Obscenity in New York City, 1909–1945*. New York: Columbia University Press, 2000.

Gertzman, Jay A. *Bookleggers and Smuthounds: The Trade in Erotica, 1920–1940*. University Park: University of Pennsylvania Press, 1999.

Gurstein, Rochelle. *The Repeal of Reticence: A History of America's Cultural and Legal Struggles over Free Speech, Obscenity, Sexual Liberation, and Modern Art*. New York: Hill and Wang, 1996.

Heins, Marjorie. *Not in Front of the Children: "Indecency," Censorship, and the Innocence of Youth.* New York: Hill and Wang, 2001.

———. *Sex, Sin, and Blasphemy: A Guide to America's Censorship Wars.* New York: The New Press, 1993, 1998.

Horowitz, Helen Lefkowitz. *Rereading Sex: Battles over Sexual Knowledge and Suppression in Nineteenth Century America.* New York: Knopf, 2002.

Hughes, Geoffrey. *Swearing: A Social History of Foul Language, Oaths, and Profanity in English.* New York: Penguin, 1991, 1998.

Hunt, Lynn, ed. *The Invention of Pornography: Obscenity and the Origins of Modernity, 1500–1800.* New York: Zone Books, 1993.

Kendrick, Walter. *The Secret Museum.* New York: Viking, 1987.

Ladenson, Elisabeth. *Dirt for Art's Sake: Books on Trial from* Madame Bovary *to* Lolita. Ithaca, NY: Cornell University Press, 2007.

Lewis, Felice Flanery. *Literature, Obscenity and Law.* Carbondale: Southern Illinois University Press, 1976.

MacKinnon, Catharine. *Feminism Unmodified: Discourses on Life and Law.* Cambridge, MA: Harvard University Press, 1987.

Mill, John Stewart. *On Liberty and Other Writings.* Ed. Stefan Collini. New York: Cambridge University Press, 1989.

Nussbaum, Martha C. *Hiding from Humanity: Disgust, Shame, and the Law.* Princeton: Princeton University Press, 2004.

Parkes, Adam. *Modernism and the Theater of Censorship.* New York: Oxford University Press, 1996.

Pease, Allison. *Modernism, Mass Culture, and the Aesthetics of Obscenity.* Cambridge: Cambridge University Press, 2000.

Peters, John Durham. *Courting the Abyss.* Chicago: University of Chicago Press, 2005.

Rembar, Charles. *The End of Obscenity.* New York: Bantam, 1968.

Stoler, Ann. "Sexual Affronts and Racial Frontiers: European Identities and the Cultural Politics of Exclusion in Colonial Southeast Asia." *Tensions of Empire: Colonial Cultures in a Bourgeois World.* Ed. Frederick Cooper and Ann Laura Stoler. Berkeley: University of California Press, 1997. 198–237.

Strossen, Nadine. *Defending Pornography, Free Speech, Sex, and the Fight for Women's Rights.* New York: Scribner's, 1995.

Weiss, Allen S. *The Aesthetics of Excess.* Albany: State University of New York Press, 1989.

Williams, Linda. *Hard Core.* Berkeley: University of California Press, 1999.

———. *Screening Sex.* Durham, NC: Duke University Press, 2008.

Contributors

ABOUT THE EDITORS

Loren Glass is Associate Professor of English at the University of Iowa. His book, *Authors Inc.: Literary Celebrity in the Modern United States, 1880–1980*, was published by New York University Press in 2004. He is currently writing a history of Grove Press.

Charles F. Williams is a doctoral candidate in American Studies at the University of Iowa. He is currently writing an intellectual genealogy of the influence of Freud's repressive theory of culture upon U.S. counter-cultural formations in the twentieth century.

ABOUT THE CONTRIBUTORS

Mikita Brottman teaches in the Department of Language, Literature and Culture at the Maryland Institute College of Art. She is author of *High Theory, Low Culture* and writes regularly for a number of publications, both mainstream and alternative; she is also a psychoanalyst in private practice.

Brett Gary is Associate Professor and Director of Graduate Studies in the Department of Media, Culture, and Communication at NYU. He is writing a history of the anti-censorship tradition in American liberalism, focusing on the work of ACLU general counsel Morris L. Ernst.

Laura Kipnis is a professor in the Radio-TV-Film Department at Northwestern. Her books include *The Female Thing: Dirt, Sex, Envy, Vulnerability; Against Love: A Polemic;* and *Bound and Gagged: Pornography and the Politics of Fantasy in America.*

Tim Miller is an internationally acclaimed performance artist, whose work explores the artistic, spiritual, and political topography of his identity as a gay man. Since 1990, he has taught performance in the theater department at UCLA and the dance program at Cal State LA. He is author of *Shirts and Skins* and *Body Blows*. In the 1990s, as one of the "NEA 4," he successfully sued the federal government for violation of his First Amendment rights.

John Durham Peters is F. Wendell Miller Distinguished Professor of Communication Studies at the University of Iowa and author of the award-winning book *Speaking into the Air*. His second book, *Courting the Abyss: Free Speech and the Liberal Tradition*, was published by the University of Chicago Press in spring 2005.

Jyoti Puri is Associate Professor of Sociology and Women's Studies at Simmons College. Her book, *Women, Body, Desire in Postcolonial India: Narratives of Gender and Sexuality*, was published by Routledge in June 1999. Her new projects include research on the emergence of sexual identities within India and a book on issues of colonialism and nationalism.

David Sterritt is chairman of the National Society of Film Critics, Professor Emeritus of Theater and Film at Long Island University, and past chair of the Columbia University Seminar on Cinema and Interdisciplinary Interpretation. His writing has appeared in *Cahiers du Cinema*, the *Journal of Aesthetics and Art Criticism*, *Cineaste*, and many other publications. His books include *The Films of Jean-Luc Godard: Seeing the Invisible* (Cambridge University Press) and *Guiltless Pleasures: A David Sterritt Film Reader* (University Press of Mississippi).

Nadine Strossen is former President of the ACLU; Professor of Law at New York Law School; and author of *Defending Pornography: Free Speech, Sex, and the Fight for Women's Rights* (NYU Press 2000) and *The Government v. Erotica: The Siege of Adam and Eve* (Prometheus 2001). She has written, lectured, and practiced extensively in the areas of constitutional law, civil liberties, and international human rights.

Michael Taussig is an Australian-born medical doctor and teaches anthropology in NYC. He writes fictocriticism. His publications include *The Devil and Commodity Fetishism in South America; Shamanism, Colonialism, and the Wild Man; The Nervous System; Mimesis and Alterity; The Magic of the State; Law in a Lawless Land;* and *My Cocaine Museum*.

Index